THE REAL CHIEF
LIAM LYNCH

THE REAL CHIEF
LIAM LYNCH

MEDA RYAN

MERCIER PRESS

Mercier Press
Douglas Village, Cork
www.mercierpress.ie

Trade enquiries to Columba Mercier Distribution,
55a Spruce Avenue, Stillorgan Industrial Park, Blackrock, Dublin

© Meda Ryan, 1986, 2005
First published 1986
This edition 2005

1 85635 460 1

10 9 8 7 6 5 4 3 2 1

Dedication
To the memory of Sheila Ryan

Printed in Ireland by ColourBooks

Contents

Acknowledgments

Without the private letters and documents given to me by Biddy O'Callaghan and her husband Thomas this book would be very different, so I am deeply indebted to them for trusting me with this material. I am also indebted to Moss O'Connor and Diarmuid Mullins who were not alone responsible for putting me in touch with Biddy O'Callaghan but in also supplying me with information which broadened the scope of my research; I am grateful to Dermot Walsh, Nick Condon and Liam Irwin who were responsible for initiating the chain of these events.

A sincere word of gratitude is due to the many who went out of their way to help in my research, people like Noel Crowley, Mary Moroney and Marie Browne of the Ennis County Library, also Thomas McCarthy, Cork City Library, the Library staff at Mary Immaculate College, Limerick; the continuous assistance of the staff in the Archives Department of University College, Dublin, and that department for the use of material, also the Mulcahy Trust for access to, and permission to quote from, the papers of Richard Mulcahy; Raymond Smith of *Independent Newspapers* for his helpful advice and assistance in research; the Library staff of the *Irish Independent* Newspapers, the *Irish Press*, the *Irish Times*, the *Cork Examiner*, the *Cork Weekly Examiner*, the *Limerick Leader*, the *Clonmel Nationalist*, the *Clonmel Chronicle*, the *Clare Champion*, the *Kerryman*, the *Southern Star* and the *Tipperary Star*; Donncha O'Dulaing of *RTÉ*, Domhnal Mac Giolla Phoil and Eily Hales McCarthy for their continuous help and encouragement; also Ned Murphy, Gus Nugent, Mick O'Neill, Jim Kearney, Bill Powell, Seán MacBride, Bill McKenna, John Flanagan, Tommy Cassidy, Con Donovan, John O'Leary, Joe Walsh, Mary Ann Nugent, Peggy Quinlan, Mike Hennessy, Gerry Smyth, Anne-Marie White, John Purcell, Sandra Alley, Maura Greene, Micheline Egan, Todd Andrews, Liam Deasy, Tom Barry, Matt Flood, Paddy O'Brien (Liscarroll) Ernest Blythe, Johnny Fanning, Madge Hales Murphy,

7

Michael Brennan, Emmet Dalton, Dan Cahalane, Seán Hyde, Frank Aiken and Pat O'Mahony.

The photographs supplied by Christy O'Callaghan, Helena O'Callaghan, Bernadette O'Connor Ó Liatháin, Pat O'Mahony, Mary O'Mahony, Frank Flynn, John Gallahue, Paddy O'Brien, Margaret O'Brien, Michael McGrath, Michael MacEvilly, Peter Somers and Con O'Donovan are an important enhancement to this book.

Grateful thanks is also due to the staff at the National Library, the Public Records Office, the British Library Board Newspaper, Clonmel County Clinic, Clonmel County Registrar's Office and Radio Telefís Éireann Sound Archives.

A sincere thank you to all at Mercier Press, and especially my editor, Mary Feehan, who worked with me through the final draft of the manuscript. A special word of gratitude is due to members of my family and to my many relatives and friends for their patience throughout my years of research and writing.

I want to thank the many people for their hospitality during the course of my research; thanks is also due to those who could not help directly but took the trouble to write or telephone explaining where information could he obtained.

Any omission in this acknowledgement has not been deliberate, as the assistance of all has been gratefully accepted.

Introduction

While working on a biography of Tom Barry I realised that he did not always see eye to eye with Liam Lynch. Both men were strong-minded Republicans, and though initially Barry's attitude was more radical than Lynch's, he was, during the closing stages of the Civil War, much more flexible. At various periods during the Civil War both men belonged to separate divisions of the same 'divide' often voting in opposition to one another.

Through working on a biography of Barry, I considered that I had come to understand the man, and, because of Barry's close links with Lynch, I felt compelled to get an insight into Lynch – the man. It was the clash of personalities, which first attracted me towards investigating the life of Liam Lynch. When I discussed the matter with Seán Feehan of Mercier Press, this compulsion crystallised and led to this biography.

Fortunately my research was aided by original material, especially the personal letters which Liam Lynch had written to his mother, his family and others. The personal correspondence (now held by Liam's niece, Biddy O'Callaghan) was invaluable, as, in his letters, he often expressed his very private thoughts. It was only possible to use a fraction of the material in these letters, but I hope that in doing so his strength of character, together with the vision, which Lynch possessed, emerges. From his letters, as well as his responses to misrepresentation of him in newspapers, it is obvious that he wanted his ideas and his intentions to be honestly interpreted. 'I do hope I shall live through this,' he wrote in a letter to his brother Tom during the Civil War, 'that future generations will have written for them the full details of all the traitorous acts.' But such was not to be; he was killed at the age of twenty-nine.

His dislike of hypocrisy is evident in both his words and actions. He always followed his beliefs and never acted through a desire for notoriety. 'Through the war I have got to understand so much of the human being,' he wrote to his mother during the truce, 'that when peace comes, I would wish for nothing more than hide myself away from all the people that know me, or even follow my dead comrades.'

During my early research I wrote to Jim Kearney, an IRA veteran, in connection with a point which I wanted clarified. In doing so I used the word 'Irregulars'. I quote from his reply: 'Irregulars! Where did you get that dirty word?' Later, I discovered Liam Lynch also detested the term, saying it was coined by pro-treatyites as a derogatory label. I have not therefore used 'Irregulars' or 'Staters' except as part of a quotation. Liam Lynch was known as 'The Chief' among Republicans, particularly in the First Southern Division. Siobhán Creedon tells a story of how Margaret Mackin came with dispatches by boat from Dublin to Cork and on to the Creedon hotel near Mallow during the Civil War. 'I have messages for the Chief,' she said. Siobhán's brother, Michael, drove the two women to headquarters where they knew an important meeting was being held. Upon arrival, Margaret had to first go into a side room to undo the dispatches, which she had stitched to her dress. Liam Deasy came out of the meeting saying that the Chief was very busy but would speak to them as soon as possible. Shortly afterwards Liam Lynch emerged, and according to Siobhán, 'Margaret stared at him in complete surprise.' Seeing that they did not appear to know each other she introduced them. 'But,' stammered Margaret, 'it was Mr de Valera I wanted!' Liam Lynch explained that De Valera was in West Cork but would be along in a few days, and that, meanwhile, he would see that the dispatches were delivered. Later, when Margaret explained her dilemma upon seeing Lynch, Siobhán responded, 'We call Liam Lynch "the Chief" – he is the real Chief! Chief of the IRA.'

In most historical books, references to Liam Lynch's death merely state that he was fatally wounded in the Knockmealdown mountains; while I accepted the straight-forward view that he died from a Free State force bullet, it was not until I began my research that I discovered a question mark hung over his death.

On 7 April 1935, Maurice Twomey (who was with Liam on the morning he was shot in the Knockmealdowns) unveiled a watch-tower memorial to him close to the spot where he fell. Since 1935 a ceremony, organised by Sinn Féin, is held there each year. And in Kilcrumper graveyard where he is buried, since 1956 another ceremony takes place on an annual basis in which some Fianna Fáil members participate. On the Sunday nearest 7 September (to commemorate the Fermoy raid in 1919) at all venues 'old IRA' veterans, together with interested members of the public, attend the organised ceremonies each year. So it has been said, 'There are two different Lynchs buried!' – ostensibly two different interpretations of the Republican vision portrayed by the one man.

It is ironic that the grand-daughter of Éamon de Valera, Síle de Valera TD in 1979, at a Liam Lynch commemorative ceremony, hastened the early resignation of the then leader of the Fianna Fáil party, Jack Lynch, when she called on him 'to demonstrate his Republicanism': but as John Bowman pointed out in his book *De Valera and the Ulster Question 1917–1973*, that, while De Valera, during the last meeting with Liam tried 'to persuade him to abandon military resistance to the Free State, Liam Lynch was concerned lest the decision reached fell short of fundamental Republicanism.'

In a letter to his brother dated 26 October 1917, Liam had expressed his opinion that it was through armed resistance that Ireland 'would achieve its Nationhood.' It was his belief that the 'army has to hew the way for politics to follow.'

Many of his comrades have wondered why Liam Lynch did not get the recognition which they felt he deserved, even though he had been offered the position as commander-in-chief of the army in December 1921; the consensus amongst his compatriots was that, in the documentation of history, De Valera overshadowed him. There is no doubt that Liam's insistence in holding out to the end, for nothing less than 'an Irish Republic' when

11

victory for that cause was becoming increasingly remote, meant that he was alienating himself from other members of the Republican Executive. However, Liam reiterated his viewpoint in a letter to his brother, dated 12 December 1921, 'As you stated, De Valera was the first to rebel.' But rebelling as a mere protest was not sufficient: 'Speeches and fine talk do not go far these days ... what we want is a definite line of action, and in going along that, to use the most effective means at our disposal.' Because of the firm stand which he took in holding out for a Republic, his deeds of bravery, especially previous to the Civil War, appear to have been downgraded, so much so that he is often mentioned as if in passing.

Yet, historically, Liam Lynch is an extremely important figure because of the part he played in gaining Irish independence – first as commander of Cork No. 2 brigade and later as commander of the First Southern Division. The part he played with Michael Collins, Richard Mulcahy, Liam Deasy, Tom Barry and others, in endeavouring to avoid Civil War, and his efforts to achieve a thirty-two county Republic for Ireland rather than a partitioned state, should not be underestimated. During the Civil War period, as chief-of-staff of the Republican forces, he was the major driving power and spokesman for that section. I believe therefore, that this is a necessary biography.

Meda Ryan

The fatal shot

Liam Lynch, chief-of-staff of the Irish Republican Army, rested with two of his travelling companions, Frank Aiken and Seán Hyde, in a house on the banks of the Tar River at the foot of the Knockmealdown mountains. It was the eve of 10 April 1923.

Before dawn they were awakened and told that Free State troops had been sighted. Liam and other members of the Executive had assembled by 5 a.m. at Houlihans, the house nearest the mountains. As they waited for further reports they sipped tea. These men were not unduly alarmed as all of them had, on more than one occasion, stood on the precipice of danger; raids of this nature were an almost daily occurrence, so believing that they had left no traces, they decided to wait.

A scout rushed in at about 8 o'clock with news that another column of Free State troops was approaching over the mountains to their left. Their line of escape was endangered. After months of Civil War, fellow members of the Republican Executive had finally persuaded Liam Lynch that a meeting was imperative, and because of this, a number of members were now caught with their backs to the mountain; Liam Lynch had always feared this type of situation. Though the Free State government was bent on crushing the 'armed revolt' and forcing the opposition into an unconditional surrender, Liam Lynch had pledged that he would not surrender:

> We have declared for an Irish Republic and will not live under any other law.[1]

Since the execution of four Republican prisoners on 8 December 1922, as a reprisal for the shooting of Seán Hales, a member of the Dáil, much of the conflict had begun to lack human dignity; the rules of war were being flouted.[2]

Already Liam Deasy, imprisoned Republican Executive member and former brigade adjutant, was compelled to avail of the only option his captors left open to him; he signed a dictated document which called on his fellow members of the Executive to agree to an unconditional surrender.[3] By January 1923 over fifty Republican prisoners had been executed and more had been sentenced to death (eventually a total of seventy-seven prisoners were shot as reprisals, though Ernest Blythe gave 85 as the number of prisoner executions).[4] Before his capture, Deasy and most of the Executive had come to the conclusion that further bloodshed would be in vain since it had become evident that for them a military victory was no longer a possibility.

However, Liam Lynch was determined that, 'the war will go on until the independence of our country is recognised by our enemies, foreign and domestic ...'[5] He was well aware that, if a meeting of the Executive was called, he would have to listen to the words 'unconditional surrender' and these were hateful to him. He had fought too hard, suffered too much, to concede all with the stroke of a pen. More than most men of the period, he had tried several avenues in order to secure a consensus in an effort to avoid Civil War. But when the break came he channelled his energies totally into the ideal of a thirty-two county Irish Republic.

Though his comrades had finally persuaded him to at least call a meeting, he had secretly confided to Seán Hyde that he would not be coerced into a surrender position.[6] This proposed meeting for 10 April 1923 was *ipso facto* the continuation of the March Executive meeting which ran for three days without reaching a consensus. Lynch, Frank Aiken and Seán Hyde had left the 'Katmandu' bunker on 4 April and had travelled mainly on foot towards the Knockmealdowns. On 10 April as he and his comrades groped their way up the mountainside the sound of gunfire forced them to quicken their pace; then there was a lull in the firing. 'For perhaps twenty seconds the still clear air of the morning was soundless, and then one single shot rang out.'

Liam Lynch fell. 'My God, I'm hit!' he cried.[7]

Over the years since that April morning in 1923 questions

have been asked about his death. It is generally accepted that it was a bullet from a Free State gun which hit him, but there are those who say that Lynch had to be removed because he was regarded as a stumbling block in any cease-fire negotiations. Was it because of the speed with which the cessation of hostilities was conducted following Liam Lynch's death that suspicion surrounded the manner in which he was killed?

As the Civil War had dragged over the winter months and Lynch had continued to believe in the possibility of victory, De Valera, Frank Aiken and others looked ahead towards some form of political recognition. Many of the anti-treatyites had come to realise the futility of the continuance of a war which pointed towards the defeat as well as the annihilation of the principal leaders. The available members met ten days after his death and unanimously elected Frank Aiken to replace Liam Lynch as chief-of-staff. They also appointed an Army Council of three (Liam Pilkington who had replaced Liam Lynch on a temporary basis; Tom Barry and Frank Aiken).

This meeting passed a resolution authorising the Republican Government and Army Council to make peace with the Free State authorities. At a meeting of the Executive and Army Council held on 26 and 27 April, over which De Valera presided, it was decided that armed resistance to the Free State forces should be terminated. A proclamation was drawn up announcing their readiness to negotiate an immediate cease-fire, and the order for the suspension of all operations from 30 April was also issued by Frank Aiken. This was just twenty days after Lynch's death. It was the initial seed-setting which led to the foundation of the Fianna Fáil political party.

So was Lynch assassinated?
Was he hit by a long-range shot fired by a member of the Free State forces?

In certain 'pockets' of the country it is said that there was an organised plot to get rid of Lynch, the belief being that 'he was a stumbling block for those of the cease-fire, dump-arms element.'

Following Liam Lynch's death an inquest was held; he was in fact a prisoner – a wounded officer who died in enemy hands, therefore and inquest was believed necessary.

Ned Murphy, a member of the Free State intelligence staff, was out on the round up with the forces on that morning. Having searched Houlihan's house for any tell-tale papers or documents, Murphy and his section climbed the mountain. He discovered Lynch, who had already been found by another Free State party and placed on a makeshift stretcher. 'My job was to collect any documents and also to file a report,' he recalled.

Ned Murphy outlined for me the final events of Lynch's life as he saw them; these are detailed, analysed and integrated with the inquest findings, newspaper reports and other interviews towards the final part of this book, consequently clarifying the source of the bullet which ended Liam Lynch's life.

Early life and vision of Ireland

In the townland of Barnagurraha, under the western slopes of the Galtee mountains, a fifth child was born to Jeremiah Lynch and Mary Kelly Lynch on 9 November 1893, and christened William Fanaghan, soon to become known as Liam.[1]

At the age of four and a half he was sent to Anglesboro school which he attended for the next twelve years. A diligent and hard-working pupil, Liam is remembered by his teacher, Patrick Kelly, as a 'mild, gentle boy above the average in intelligence'.

From early childhood, young Liam was aware of the hardships undertaken to make a living off the land; he was also aware of the difficulties under which ownership of the land had been secured. From his home north of Mitchelstown, in the Cork/Limerick border, he could view the Aherlow River, Paradise Hill, and the towering Galtees. Here in this rich fertile land he learned how his ancestors secured their holdings through sweat and blood. His home, like most of those in the rural Ireland of his day, was a centre of history and storytelling. Families and neighbours would gather round the fireside and tell of the background to their existence, and the long history of the struggle for freedom.

The Lynchs lived in the fertile plain known as Feara Muighe Feine with the royal seat and capital at Glanworth. This was later Desmond land, parcelled out after the confiscation, when thousands of acres were given to Elizabethan adventurers, on condition that it should be planted with English settlers. After Irish natives had been driven from their holdings by the sword, six thousand acres of this rich land was granted to an Arthur Hyde, for which he paid one penny per acre upon undertaking to plant it with English subjects. (One branch of the Hyde family gave us Douglas Hyde, the founder of the Gaelic League and first president of Ireland.)

One of the dispossessed families was a Lynch. Though there is no record how this family survived for five generations, they, like some families who were not among those banished in Cromwell's 'to Hell or to Connaught' dictum, were forced to tolerate being in servitude to the planters. Gradually they achieved tenancy of a small holding from the new landlords. They were in servitude, without rights, property and for a time without legal existence. But they inherited a Gaelic culture and Gaelic tradition. It was into this Liam Lynch was born. His uncle, John Lynch with William Condon rode on horseback to Kilmallock for the Easter Rising. The MacNeill cancellation and the surrounding of the town meant they had to return home. His mother, Mary Kelly had been joint secretary of the Ballylanders Branch of the Ladies' Land League. Hannah Cleary, his godmother was a Fenian and great storyteller with a wide knowledge of history.

Young Liam Lynch learned that the family farm had been acquired through great sacrifice. This understanding of his background would one day cause him to lead the men and women of south Munster in a fight which would finally destroy the last remnants of the plantation and so give the Irish people control over their own destiny.

At the age of nine, investigations revealed that he had defective eyesight, consequently he had to leave school for a short time to have treatment in Cork and had to wear glasses for the remainder of his life. Being particularly attracted to deeds of bravery, as a child, Liam on one occasion climbed, with some of his school companions, to the top of the Galtymore Mountains pointing northwards to Ballyneety. He spontaneously rendered an accurate account of Patrick Sarsfield's famous night ride and destruction of the Williamite siege train. Years later he referred to this again in a letter to his brother Tom.[2]

In 1910 at the age of seventeen the shy retiring Liam left home and entered upon a three years apprenticeship term at the hardware trade of Mr P. O'Neill. During this time he acquired a great taste for reading and especially for books of Irish historical

Mary Kelly-Lynch, Liam Lynch's mother (died 1937)
(Courtesy, Pat & Mary O'Mahony)

Jeremiah Lynch, Liam Lynch's father (died 5 June 1914)
(Courtesy, Pat & Mary O'Mahony)

Three brothers: (left to right) *Fr Tom Lynch, Brother Martin P. Lynch, Liam Lynch*
(Courtesy, Christy O'Callaghan)

Liam Lynch, 1918
(Courtesy, Pat & Mary O'Mahony)

interest. In Mitchelstown he joined the Gaelic League and the Ancient Order of Hibernians and continued his education by joining a technical class. Every Sunday, he returned to his parents' home at Barnagurraha. In 1914 his father Jeremiah died. Liam was just twenty-one.

Fermoy was a garrison town. It held a larger concentration of British troops than any other town in the county. Kilworth and Moorepark camps contained strong elements of British-Union units. Union Jacks, khaki and recruiting oratory for the British army were very much in evidence. Many young men joined the British army, believing as they had been told, that they were fighting for the freedom of small nations including their own; however, many also questioned this military regime and some, like Liam Lynch, questioned the military strength of a foreign power whose troops occupied his own country. Liam was an avid reader of newspapers, and keenly interested in events abroad. Friends said of him 'he watched everything and everybody to see where was truth and where was sincerity'. He might have remained an observer were it not for an event subsequent to the 1916 Easter Week Rising which caused him to change his life.

Forty-six organised companies in Cork city and county, though poorly armed, believed that they were denied participation in the 1916 events when they accepted MacNeill's cancellation of all parades that Easter. Because of participation in the volunteers, some families or individuals were singled out for harassment. The Kents of Fermoy who had been active in the volunteers were the first family to receive a backlash. Thomas, David, Richard and William Kent had not been sleeping at home since the Easter Rising, but on 1 May returned to spend their first night at home.

Early the following morning, the house was surrounded by armed police who said they had orders to arrest the entire family. The Kents armed with a rifle and three shotguns decided to resist. An open conflict ensued when the police opened fire and continued until the defenders had exhausted their ammunition; by this time the police had called in military reinforcements. When the family surrendered, David was seriously wounded, Thomas was immediately handcuffed and not allowed put on his boots, whilst Richard, an athlete, made a bid to escape, but in doing so was mortally wounded.

Liam Lynch was standing on Fermoy bridge that morning when he saw the Kent family having been arrested by British soldiers. Young Thomas was in his bare feet, William and their mother were prisoners and a horse was drawing a cart on which Richard and David lay wounded. Richard was to die two days later at the hands of his captors and Thomas would, within a week face the British firing squad in Cork. It was a scene, which cut to Liam's very heart, and he associated it with the horror of the executions in Dublin about which he had read. That night he made a resolution that he 'would atone as far as possible to dedicate his life for the sacrifices of the martyred dead': he was determined that he would make the Irish Republic a reality; he was now a man of 'one allegiance only', believing that the only way to achieve freedom was by force, that it was in arms and only in arms that Ireland would achieve liberty.[3]

From then on, he did not deviate from his aim, which he pursued with single-minded tenacity and devotion. For this tall, sturdy, agile young man, the action taken by the volunteers in the GPO during Easter Week was a spark which lit the flame to his future. He saw the history of the long struggle of the Irish people for liberty with a new vision. With his brother Tom, who was then a clerical student in Thurles, he would often talk with pride about the events of Easter Week and would speak of the men who fought for Ireland's freedom. In their intimate conversations he would discuss methods of achieving this freedom for the Irish nation.

As time progressed Liam talked not of dying for Ireland but of living and working for Ireland. His was a logical mind; as a young boy he was an excellent draughts player, quick to see the weakness in an opponent's position and equally he quickly availed of the advantage. Similar characteristics were evident in his subsequent task of commanding the volunteer force. He was a deep thinker and in the volunteers he saw the raw material which could, if properly forged, become a powerful weapon. Knowing that loyalty and idealism were not enough, he favoured cool, calculated planning coupled with an organised approach to the military problem. In the aftermath of Easter Week, following the arrest of leaders who were deported to internment camps in England, the volunteer organisation disintegrated in many parts of the country. Upon the release of internees at Christmas, and of sentenced prisoners in June 1917, the country was ready for vigorous organisations.

Like many a young man at the time, Liam Lynch took a keen interest in these developments. He had wanted to meet somebody who had taken part in the 1916 Rising and hear the exact details. An occasion presented itself when a farmer from the Galtees told him that he had one of the men who took part in the Rising staying with him. Liam made arrangements to meet the man who was 'on the run'. He was both surprised and delighted to learn that it was another Galtee man, a neighbour, Donal O'Hannigan. Liam immediately brought him home to his mother at Barnagurraha where he stayed for some time. Liam, still working in Fermoy, visited them frequently and when his brother Tom returned from college, the three met and talked about Ireland's future. Like many an Irishman, he hoped that the peace conference due to take place at the end of the war would give Ireland's claim for independence a favourable hearing, yet he was not prepared to rely on the possibility. He wrote to his brother in October 1917, 'I as well as thousands of others are preparing hard to mount whatever breach is allotted to us ... If we do not get what is our own at the peace conference we will have to fight for it. In a few months we will be able to marshal an army.'[4]

By this time the organisation of that army had begun on a country-wide basis. Companies were being formed, officers elected and elementary training in voluntary discipline was being organised. When the Irish Volunteer Company at Fermoy was re-organised in early 1917 Liam Lynch was elected first lieutenant.

Declaration for an Irish Republic

When De Valera was returned in the Clare election of June 1917 with an overwhelming majority it was a clear indication of the mood of the people and their endorsement of the aims of the 1916 men. At the October Sinn Féin Ard Fheis 1,200 Cumann throughout the country unanimously adopted a constitution, the preamble to which declared:

> Sinn Féin aims at securing the international recognition of Ireland as an Independent Irish Republic. Having achieved that status the Irish people may by referendum freely choose their own form of government.

At this Ard Fheis, Éamon de Valera was elected president and at the volunteer convention on 27 October, he was also elected president of that body. By being president of the two principal organisations it seemed as if the nation had found a leader; the way was open for the great national movement.

British proclamations of 1 August 1917 prohibited the wearing of military uniform or the carrying of hurleys. On 15 August that same year volunteers were arrested on a large scale throughout the country. This was followed by a hunger-strike. Among the hunger-strikers was Thomas Ashe, who was forcibly fed and died on 25 September 1917. This created disquiet among the volunteers, so the volunteer Executive decided to challenge the British prohibition and ordered parades in uniform to be held throughout the country on Sunday 21 October.

On that day Liam Lynch in volunteer uniform was second in command of the sixty-seven men of Fermoy company who marched out to meet the RIC. Happy with the challenge, Liam wrote to his brother of the two hours drilling: 'We are to keep drilling until the last man is gone. We mean to break the law of

Éamon de Valera

illegal drilling.' He also warned his brother who was in Thurles College that he was to write on 'friendly matters' only as his letters were being read in the post office. He thought that he might be arrested – judging by a letter to his brother on 1 November, he appears to have been disappointed that he was not arrested. His brother however, advised 'that though it was honourable and good to go to gaol it would be better for the lads to stay out, work harder and give England something livelier than gaol work.' From then on he was not anxious for imprisonment but he did warn his brother, 'I am only doing my duty to God and my country.'

Liam O'Denn, the company captain was arrested and Liam was given his place in command of the company. Each Sunday, parades continued and generally when a company captain was arrested another was ready to take his place. Liam Lynch's philosophy is well expressed in one of his letters:

> We have declared for an Irish Republic and will not live under any other law.[1]

As far as he was concerned Britain could not defeat them except by interning the whole volunteer force. He told his brother in a letter on 9 November: 'Our parade was not prevented last Sunday but we had made arrangements to carry on elsewhere if such happened. We marched to Ballyhooley with about 100 volunteers where we met Glanworth, Glenville, Rathcormac and Ballyhooley volunteers – in all about 300, and I had the honour to be at their head.'[2]

One of his principal aims now was to get military training. He even had the mistaken impression that prisoners in Cork jails were getting some form of military training. In a letter to his brother he wrote: 'I would want to go there at least for a few weeks' training.'[3] He tried to lay his hands on any books that might help him to study military drilling and leadership. He even studied the guerrilla tactics of the Boars in the South African war. He was, however, aware of the surrounding problems in the heavily garrisoned town of Fermoy and he was also aware that, apart from the military parades which they held on Sundays, his group was practically unarmed; they were untrained, had no military assets except a sturdy manhood and a glowing faith in the justice of their cause.

In mid December, when Éamon de Valera came to speak at a public meeting in Fermoy, Liam, dressed in uniform, paraded at the head of the local company to welcome him.

The Fermoy battalion was the sixth of the brigade's twenty battalions at that time.[4] (Battalion commandant was Martin O'Keefe; vice commandant, Michael Fitzgerald; adjutant, Liam Lynch; quarter-master, George Power.) Being elected battalion adjutant gave Liam a wider scope for his activities. A diligent worker, by setting a standard in his own work, he showed what could be achieved. He made it his business to visit one company each week and to study their problems – he urged perfection and impressed on his comrades the importance of the acquisition of arms.

The threat of conscription to the British army hardened the temper of the people against British rule; it also meant that the volunteer movement gained more support from the population. Volunteering had become respectable. Because of the threat of conscription Liam left his place of employment in April 1918. With Michael Fitzgerald, Larry Condon and George Power he devoted himself full time to preparing for active service. By the summer of 1918 he had the first mobilisation unit in active operation.

The British authorities now invented a mythical German plot to justify large-scale arrests of volunteers and Sinn Féin leaders. Apparently, the idea was to deprive the people of leadership, which would, in turn, weaken the national morale. Arrests were made on 17 and 18 May 1918 when seventy-three people were deported to England. As Liam had already left his place of employment he escaped arrest.

He now decided that more arms should be secured for his

battalion. Upon receipt of information that, on a certain date, a train, carrying arms, would travel from Mallow to Fermoy, Liam, with the aid of Liam Tobin, mobilised about fifty men between Ballyhooley and Castletownroche to ambush the train. Nothing was left to chance. Wires were cut, cars were mobilised to remove the expected arms captured and the arrangements for their safe disposal was organised. The train was held up and searched, but contained no arms. Nevertheless, as far as Liam was concerned, the effort gave the battalion valuable experience.

Following this episode, Tomás MacCurtain, lord mayor of Cork, visited the battalion and gave Liam instructions which were to be implemented in the event of any enforcement of conscription. Any local problems or any difficulties which might arise in each area were to be dealt with by the brigade and battalion officers. In the Cork brigade it was visualised that the entire force might be called out on active duty, consequently detailed instruction on discipline and on problems of billeting and feeding were issued. Liam outlined a list of activities: cyclist-dispatch riders to man a communication system were established and tested.

An editorial in An tÓglach, September 1918 read, 'The unanimous decision of the Executive of the Irish volunteers is to resist conscription to the death with all the military force and warlike resources at our command.'[5] How could a group of men resist force without ammunition and without trained leaders? Headquarters were unable to help. In the absence of arms and ammunition the only immediate advice Liam could give the men was to use pitch forks or whatever was available in the face of aggression; other means could afterwards be pursued.

Liam realised what the task of feeding, clothing and finding shelter for a volunteer force would involve. He also realised that such a force could become an unruly mob, therefore it was important that morale be sustained and that communications be kept at a high level. Now, more that ever, he realised that the acquisition of arms was of paramount importance. Given arms other difficulties could be overcome.

The war in Europe ended on 11 November 1918 and with it the threat of conscription. A young volunteer army had stood together and had won a significant and bloodless victory. Since February, the carrying of arms had been prohibited, and from June onwards a series of proclamations was designed by the authorities to destroy national organisations. Arrests were numerous, creating problems for many units of the volunteers. There was continuous resistance by hunger-strikers in the jails. In addition GHQ issued a policy of resistance on 20 August 1918 ordering the volunteers, when brought to trial, to refuse to recognise the jurisdiction of the court.

Cork County had, by mid 1918, re-organised under the direction of the vigorous Tomás MacCurtain, the brigade commandant.[6] All GHQ could do was issue general directions and allow each area under their commanders to shape their army. Many who had joined because of the threat of conscription began to drop out and because there were more men available and willing to fight than there were weapons to arm them, morale began to drop. However, Liam continued to drill the men every Sunday and on certain weekdays. He kept impressing on the Fermoy battalion that their objective was 'a military victory' and that if the volunteer army did not stick together now and fight, all hope of attaining a Republic would be lost to their generation.

A turning point in Irish history came about through the results of a general election in December 1918. The result, which became available on 28 December showed that, of 105 seats in the whole country, Republicans had captured 73. This was seen as an endorsement of the 1916 men's action and it strengthened the morale of the volunteers. The Irish people, it seemed, had declared themselves for an Irish Republic, consequently the way was opened to them for further action if the need arose. Liam Lynch, like many other officers, realised that the organisation could not be kept going indefinitely without activity and neither could they be properly trained without the use of arms.

Home Rule, which looked imminent before the Great War, had been suspended for its duration, but it was not honoured when the war ended.

At this stage GHQ decided that Cork would be divided into three brigade areas.[7] On 6 January 1919 a meeting of officers from the battalion forming the Cork No. 2 brigade was held in Batt Walshe's house in Glashbee, Mallow. The brigade was formed into seven battalions with Liam unanimously elected as brigade commandant.[8] Once the conscription crisis ended he went back to his normal employment at Barry's in Fermoy. Following the meeting and Liam's election, his brother Tom visited him and found him in an extremely happy mood, but Tom, fearful of what future events might bring, anxiously asked if he realised the full extent of his responsibilities. Liam confidently replied, 'I'll be able for it. There is great scope.' His life and his life's ambition, as far as he was concerned, was only beginning.[9]

Group photograph taken at rear of the office of the Freeman's Journal *in Dublin*
Front row: *Tadhg Barry, Tomás Mac Curtain, Pat Higgins*
Back row: *Dáithi Mac Coitir, Seán Murphy, Donal Barrett, Terence MacSwiney, Paddy Trahey*
(Courtesy, Cork Public Museum)

Love and marriage postponed for Roisín Dubh

The first Dáil Éireann assembled in the Mansion House, Dublin, on 21 January 1919. Every elected representative was invited to be present but only the Republicans attended. Of the seventy-three, thirty-four, including De Valera and Griffith, were 'absent' in jail. The Dáil was declared an illegal assembly; prohibition by the British parliament necessitated its members holding meetings in secret.

On 21 January also Séamus Robinson, Dan Breen and the other volunteers from Tipperary ambushed some council men who, escorted by police, were taking gelignite to a quarry. Two policemen were shot and the cargo secured.

As the RIC (Royal Irish Constabulary) scoured the country and arrested volunteers and Sinn Féin members, it became obvious that the British government wanted these new-found 'troublemakers' in custody.

Soon Liam Lynch took the decision to recondition his brigade. With unswerving zeal, he visited his battalion every Sunday afternoon and made personal contact with almost every officer under his command, and also with the large numbers of volunteers in all parts of his area. Wherever he went, men were impressed by his dignified soldierly stature, his sincerity, his understanding and above all his enthusiasm. His outlook was positive and he tended to think highly of most people. He had a stubborn strength and determination, which was not apparent at first sight. This helped him to forge ahead and give himself unreservedly to the service and the cause of freedom. Fluent in speech he would on occasion, when angry, stutter over a word, but this was balanced by his foresight and original, constructive opinions; men felt it an honour to serve under him. He was adaptable, quick-witted and shrewd, with a broad vision and balanced judgement.

Liam Lynch was now twenty-five. A man with a creative mind, imagination and foresight, he could accurately sum up a situation and be relied on to use sound judgement when faced with the unexpected. His approach was always thorough and methodical. He was alert to the many problems his battalion might encounter when involved in open combat. One of his comrades Paddy O'Brien described him as 'an able, active, unselfish worker for the cause; his heart and soul was in everything he did. He was in all respects, a true leader, a born leader'. As time progressed, his leadership qualities became more evident despite his shyness. 'His dynamic personality was the driving force which compelled all of us in the volunteers to get things done, and done effectively,' said Matt Flood, who had been on active service in the British army and whose expertise Liam sought to coach the members of the battalion in the correct use of weaponry.

At council meetings he was always careful to listen to all opinions and to take notes; those present found that he never interrupted the programme but would discuss whatever had arisen before the meeting closed. Though often ready to make allowances, he was intolerant of slackness or negligence. He initiated a unique system of asking for improvement with suggestions in writing from volunteers, so that the organisation could develop its fitness for battle and work in an all-round spirit of friendliness. He was quick to give credit for useful suggestions and would put them into operation when possible. At conferences he tried to express the importance of a resumption of the armed conflict.

His life was now dedicated to his volunteer work to the exclusion of all other interests. He attended every meeting and every parade. 'Sometimes he would wake one of us in the middle of the night to discuss a problem. He used to say that his brain appeared to be on fire and he couldn't sleep,' Paddy O'Brien recalls.

From his earliest association with the volunteers he had thought of Ireland in terms of a nation as a whole. Taking a broad view, he made contacts and exchanged ideas with a neighbouring command. In the early days he made frequent visits to the brigade officers in the other Cork areas, also Limerick, Waterford and Tipperary; at great personal risk he continued to visit headquarters in Dublin. Some of his comrades said he had 'a type of missionary zeal' – a thinker who looked beyond the conflict of the day, and yet a soldier. 'Thoughts of love and marriage he put aside so that nothing might stand between him and complete dedication in service to the duties he envisaged, although the love and prayers of a devoted lady went with him through all the days of strife, constant and faithful to the end he was not indifferent.'[1]

Bridie Keyes, a vibrant, dynamic young girl whom he met through Irish classes, would remain faithful to him. He had begun learning Irish seriously, and was making great progress, but because 'the tempo' of the movement had increased he couldn't continue, but he did complete the first course. Seán Ó Tuama responding to his query on the best method of becoming fluent in Irish, suggested six months in the Gaeltacht when hostilities had ceased. Liam said he would do that. Later he told Siobhán Creedon that he had 'done one thing anyway', he had got Bridie Keyes to continue to attend these Irish classes in Fermoy.

During this period, Conradh na Gaeilge often ran ceilís and concerts in Mallow. At these, false names were always given by the men and the women who were in the 'movement'. According to Siobhán Creedon (one of the organisers), 'Liam was tall, handsome and very distinguished looking; we had many enquiries as to who he was.' He was teased 'relentlessly' about this and George Power and Maurice Twomey who worked with him 'got a lot of quiet fun about the ladies' interest in him'. However, there was just the one girl to whom he was particularly attracted. 'I am doing a great line these times,' he wrote to his brother.[2] Periodically, he would meet her, and when he did, their courtship was often brief, though there were times when he talked 'through his problems' with her. These periods of intimacy went on for hours, eating into his time of sleep in one of his many hide-outs. Then as a precautionary measure they postponed seeing each other.

Some weeks after the course finished Liam told George Power that he wanted to meet Bridie Keyes again. George, with Siobhán Creedon, decided that they would get her to come to Creedon's home, so they arranged for a visit one Sunday afternoon. George and Siobhán laid plans, checked railway time-tables and made contact with Liam's friends in Fermoy. Then on 'a fresh early autumn Sunday' in 1919, George Power brought Bridie from Mallow station to the Creedon's home in Mourne Abbey. Liam was there. Bridie was, according to Siobhán Creedon, a tall, attractive-looking girl, 'very elegant in navy and white, and like Liam, gentle and quietly spoken. After lunch, she and Liam walked on the farm through our beloved Glen, while George and the family talked and told stories in the kitchen. When Liam and Bridie returned tea was ready. There was little talk during tea and when George left with Bridie for the train, Liam went to work on a pile of papers in the parlour. Somehow the bright, golden evening had lost its sparkle, and the feeling of deep sorrow stole over it. George returned and went straight away to work with Liam. In their usual fashion, they worked until suppertime.'

Speaking of marriage in a letter to Tom, his brother, Liam said, 'my whole time is required by Old Ireland.'[3]

Siobhán and George never discussed that day again. 'We both knew that these two wonderful people has postponed their happiness' to serve Ireland's need. 'A lovely young girl had had to give her place to mother Ireland,' according to Siobhán who believed that, 'the sacrifice made by Bridie Keyes was total. She was never to know the fulfilment of her dream of happiness, but was to take her place with Sarah Curran, and with the generations of Irish women who stood aside for the cause of Roisín Dubh.'[4]

14 · 11 · 23

Below: *Liam's mother,
wrote these lines in Bridie
Keyes' autograph book
(Courtesy, Christy
O'Callaghan)*

'*Easter Sunday, 1925.*

*Your memory dwells with
    brave
The faithful and the few
You hold today a Martyr's
    grave
For being Ireland true.*

Mary Lynch'

Liam Lynch
(Courtesy, Mossie O'Connor)

Above: *Introduction to
autograph book
of Bridie Keyes [Liam
Lynch's fianceé]
(Courtesy, Christy
O'Callaghan)*

'19.11.'23

*The heights of great men
    reached and kept
Were not attained by
    sudden flight
But they while their
    companions slept
Were toiling upwards in
    the night.*'

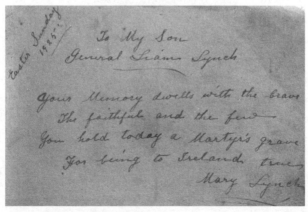

Military activity continues

Liam Lynch's dedication to the cause of an Irish Republic never wavered. One of his companions said that 'when at times he would get a little ruffled, he somehow was capable of not allowing this to take precedence. At all times, he tried to be cool and calm and calculated so that nothing would cloud his judgement.'[1]

Liam did not allow the policy of terror (burnings, lootings, torture of prisoners, execution of innocent people) to adversely influence his own actions. He expressed his belief 'that the service of freedom only stood below the service of God.' He was, however, now finding it difficult to see a way forward, and he had the additional burden of being pressed to action by men who felt they had been cheated of an opportunity in 1916. With this in mind, Liam visited Dublin in April 1919 to put forward some proposals for the Cork No. 2 brigade and to try to get some arms. He got a few revolvers, but, to his disappointment, did not get any rifles. It became quite clear to him that the Cork brigades, if they wanted to get involved in any action, would have to arm themselves by capturing arms from the enemy.

All southern brigades now put pressure on GHQ to approve a policy of attacks on British garrison forces in order to acquire arms, as there seemed to be no other prospect of obtaining them. The destiny of the volunteer movement rested on the turn of such events, and it was officers like Liam Lynch who initiated such a move. It depressed him that GHQ would not take any great responsibility and were not forthcoming with any ideas for the securing of arms. He wanted a defined policy because he felt that without one, it would be difficult to maintain discipline. Raids had taken place in other parts of Cork, particularly in the Third West Cork brigade area where rifles had been captured, therefore he felt this policy should become more widespread.

Early in 1919 Con Leddy who was O/C of Araglin company

came to Barry's of Fermoy where Liam worked and requested a raid on Araglin barracks. Liam made the inspection and obtained sanction from GHQ. On Sunday morning 20 April 1919, when three of the four RIC men occupying the barracks were at mass, a party of seven volunteers approached the building from the rear. When the constable, who was the only occupant of the post, went out for a bucket of water the volunteers entered and, on his return, held him up. He reacted quickly, and threw the bucket of water at them. He then ran down the yard and shouted, he gave the impression he was armed and he would shoot all of them. However, Liam and the other volunteers cleared the barracks of its arms, ammunition, equipment and documents – everything of military value was removed. The unarmed constable afterwards expressed thanks to the volunteers for the way they had treated him and he never subsequently attempted to identify them.

On 13 May 1919 Seán Hogan of the Third Tipperary brigade was rescued from a police escort at Knocklong railway station. The two volunteers, Ned O'Brien and Jim Scanlon who were wounded during the rescue came into Ballyporeen in the Mitchelstown area where a doctor attended them and they were given accommodation. This brought intensive raiding by the British forces to Cork No. 2 area. Liam asked Tom Kavanagh to drive him at night to Ballyporeen where they picked up the two passengers and set out for a house near Tallow. They avoided Mitchelstown, but, as they passed by Moorepark Camp outside Fermoy, a sentry challenged them. Liam determined to get through, ordered Tom to drive on. The sentry fired, but the occupants of the car escaped injury and got to William Aherne, a chemist, who dressed the men's wounds. Then Liam arranged for the men's protection; because of continuous raiding, he had them moved several times while they were recuperating.

He had been to Dublin headquarters at the end of April 1919 to obtain sanction for activities in his brigade. Now he decided to contact Cork No. 1 brigade in order to co-ordinate acti-

vities. In July, HQ informed him that he could disarm any milli-
tary party, provided there were no casualties. He could now
organise an open attack on British military forces by striking at
the core of the enemy's most powerful stronghold in Fermoy, his
brigade area. (British forces had 4,300 military and approximately 490 armed police within his brigade area).[2]

The police, who had an intimate knowledge of the population, had been keeping a close watch on activities. These opposing forces were housed in well-fortified and comfortable barracks. The ranks included officers who were experienced veterans of the European war and most of the troops had received adequate military training. They were armed with modern weapons
and backed by administrative and supply services on a war footing. In contrast, Liam Lynch had under his command 3,800
partially-trained volunteers, none on whole-time active service.
They were, nevertheless, excellently organised, efficient, disciplined and responsible, but they had no pay, no barracks with
supply services; they had only their own clothing, and were under
continuous pressure trying to meet and train in secret. They had
no heavy weapons and their arms consisted of a dozen or so rifles,
some of doubtful reliability and less than 100 revolvers and
pistols. Their back-up services (engineers, signallers, transport, intelligence and medical) were mainly non-professionals. However, what they lacked in material needs they made up for by
courage and determination, with the addition of one vital element which the enemy did not have – the backing of the people.

Liam meticulously planned his first trial of strength against
the enemy. On Sundays an armed party of British soldiers attended service at the Wesleyan church about a half a mile from
their barracks which was situated at the eastern end of Fermoy.
Liam did not know whether or not the rifles they carried were
loaded, consequently he decided they would carry out the raid
under the assumption that they were loaded. On Sunday morning 7 September 1919, fourteen soldiers with a corporal in charge,
left their barracks and marched through the town towards the

Wesleyan church. In the vicinity of the church about twenty-five volunteers from Fermoy company with six serviceable revolvers between them assembled in groups of twos and threes. Larry Condon was in charge of the main attacking party, which included John Fanning, Michael Fitzgerald, Patrick Aherne and James Fitzgerald. Liam had detailed other groups to collect the rifles and rush them to the waiting car. The rest were to close in from the rear and prevent the British getting back to their barracks. The unarmed volunteers carried short clubs concealed in their coat sleeves. George Power was in charge of one car, which stood near the church, and with another man pretended to fix the car. Behind the British party another car moved up Patrick Street; this car, which carried Liam, was to increase its speed and arrive at the church at the same time as the British forces. So far, everything was going according to plan.

Liam had given much thought to the selection of officers and men for this raid. Because it was to take place in daylight it was inevitable that well-known local officers and men taking part would afterwards have to go 'on the run' to evade arrest. Local people, especially those with cars were needed in case of casualties. Because the men under Liam's command were poorly armed at the time, speed was an integral part of the operation. Though the brunt of the action was borne by the Fermoy company, Liam sought help from other companies. Four men travelled with George Power from Mallow.[3] Jack Mulvey of Rathcormac gave his own Ford car and brought four men from the Ballynoe company.[4] Martin O'Keefe and Willie O'Mahony of Ballynoe travelled on bicycles. Pax Whelan, of the Waterford brigade, gave a third car, which also carried two volunteers – George Lenihan and Mick Mansfield. (The driver, not a volunteer, became suspicious shortly after their arrival in Fermoy and headed back for Dungarvan before the action took place.)

The military arrived at the church at the same time as Liam's car. Liam blew a whistle and called on the party to surrender. They prepared to resist. The volunteers rushed them. Shots were fired and for a minute there was a confused struggle. Liam jumped for a rifle on the road, slipped and fell. A military man who rushed him swinging a rifle butt, was shot down. Liam picked up the rifle. In a short time, the struggle was over. Fifteen rifles were loaded into one car, which was then driven up the Tallow/ Lismore road, its occupants could hear the bugle call in the barracks. The volunteers on foot scattered quickly. One of the military had been killed and three wounded. The response to the barracks' alarm was so immediate and within five minutes, two lorries carrying military were tearing out the Lismore road. This eventuality had been foreseen, therefore at Carrickbuick, a mile and a quarter from the town, two roadside trees had been partly sawn through and held in position by ropes. Under cover volunteers waited for the cars carrying the rifles to pass, immediately they knocked the trees across the road, forcing the pursuing military to detour and lose the trail.

It was only when Liam got into the car that he realised he had been wounded. He had received a bullet close to the shoulder: however, the injury did not appear to be serious. A Fermoy chemist's assistant, William Aherne, had been recruited and as they drove he treated the wounded as best he could. Liam Lynch, six men and the rifles were taken by Leo O'Callaghan in the Buick and Mulvey took five volunteers with him in the Ford.[5] A short distance out Power and Hegarty left the second car and made their way back into the town through the fields. At Kilmagner, five miles from Fermoy, the rifles were taken to a pre-arranged dump.[6] The Buick went on to Youghal, leaving Liam at Furry Hill about two miles outside the town. William Aherne 'walked into the town and called on Miss O'Keefe a member of Cumann na mBan. She informed the Youghal company officers, who brought Liam on foot to Thomas O'Connor's where his wound was dressed by Dr Michael Twomey.'[7] Meanwhile, a large scale round up by the military took place in Youghal town, but the men for whom they were searching were in safe hiding.

Because of the Fermoy action, an intensive search by the

police continued throughout the day. All neighbouring police and military posts were notified and parties of British lorries scoured the countryside. Numerous people were questioned and cars were held up, a local matchmaking party was raided and innocent people were brutalised and beaten with butts of rifles. This was a foretaste of the brutality that many citizens would experience later. The following night the East Kent regiment turned out in force and wrecked Fermoy town. Two days later the district was proclaimed a military area.

Following a message sent to Pax Whelan of Waterford, Liam was collected by car and taken a mile outside Dungarvan where Phil O'Donnell and Paddy Lynch met him; they took him to Brodericks and then to Cooneys at Carrigroe where he stayed for about two weeks; his wounds were dressed daily by Dr Moloney and he was nursed by the boxer and first aid man, Dan Cooney. From there he was taken in a pony and trap to James Kirwin's on the slopes of the Comeragh Mountains.

Liam sent word to George Power to come and see him. After this meeting at Brodericks in Dungarvan Liam returned to Cooneys for another three weeks. By this time his wound was healing very well and he was moved again to Gerry Kirwin's who had an excellent library, with several books on Irish history.

Liam, anxious that his family would know exactly where he was, sent Gerry Kirwin to Clonmel to ask his brother, Martin, to visit him, which he did the following Saturday. Liam, conscious of the approval of his family, wondered what his mother's feelings were and also what the other members of his family were saying about his involvement in the movement. Martin reassured him of their approval and gave him full details.

A few months after the Fermoy raid, feeling fit again, he returned to his brigade. On 15 November 1919, in a letter to his brother Tom he expressed a note of triumph to be conveyed to Martin who was sympathetic to his cause. 'Whatever happens now after years will justify our cause.'

Liam Lynch, with some of his division staff and officers of the brigades included in the First Southern Division, who attended as delegates to the army convention at the Mansion House, Dublin on 9 April 1922
Front row (L to R): *Seán Lehane, Tom Daly, Florrie O'Donoghue, Liam Lynch, Liam Deasy, Seán Moylan, John Joe Rice, Humphrey Murphy*
Second row: *Denis Daly, Jimmy O'Mahony, George Power, Michael Murphy, Eugene O'Neill, Seán MacSwiney, Dr Pat O'Sullivan, Jim Murphy, Moss Donegan, Gerry Hannifin*
Third row: *Jeremiah Riordan, Michael Crowley, Dan Shinnick, Con Leddy, Con O'Leary, Tom Hales, Jack O'Neill, Seán McCarthy, Dick Barrett, Andy Cooney*
Fourth row: *Tom Ward, John Lordan, Gibbs Ross, Tadgh Brosnan, Dan Mulvihill, Denis McNeilus*
Back row: Con Casey, Pax Whelan, Tom McEllistrim, Michael Harrington
(Courtesy, Cork Public Museum)

Talks with Michael Collins and GHQ

The fight for Irish independence had truly begun, but it was encountering extensive opposition. The *Cork Examiner*, which had the widest circulation in Liam's brigade area, maintained an editorial line of despair during the three vital years of struggle. Apart from a few individual priests, the clergy opposed the volunteers. The majority of the bishops spoke out strongly against the early military activities. High on the list of clergy to disapprove was His Lordship, Most Rev. Dr Coholan of Cork. This caused much pain and heart-searching. For the average volunteer, disobedience to the teaching of his spiritual advisors was at stake, but each balanced this against an even stronger belief in justice. In spite of the men's strong religious feelings, they were prepared to continue the struggle even under the threat of excommunication, particularly in the dioceses of Cork. Liam noted the discipline, steadfastness and the absolute loyalty of the men under his command.

Numerous arrests followed the Fermoy action. The local Fermoy battalion commandant Michael Fitzgerald, vice-commandant Larry Condon and company captain John Fanning were arrested. Two months later further arrests took place in Mallow.[1]

On the day of the Fermoy incident a car-load of people not connected with the attack travelled to Fermoy to attend a Sinn Féin function. When this car was traced the men faced arrest, but the head constable of the RIC, Constable D. Sullivan, who had given forty years service to the force, refused to arrest them, as from his investigation, 'there was no evidence whatsoever to connect them with the affair.' Despite his insistence, the men were arrested and Constable Sullivan was dismissed and given sixteen days to get his family and furniture out of the barracks, despite his years of service and unblemished record.

Intensive searching by the police did not deter Liam Lynch from maintaining his contacts and carrying out his duties. Following the Fermoy incident the police pledged a substantial reward for his arrest and gave an accurate description of him in their 'Police Notice'.[2]

Back in Fermoy Liam set up brigade HQ at Glenville about ten miles south-west of Fermoy. Due to arrests, several adjustments were required in the appointment of staff.[3] Liam, no longer in employment, gave his full time and energy to his work; he toured the brigade area and paid special attention to the battalion at the western end. Christmas (1919) was approaching and Liam felt he would be unable to be with his family, so he wrote to his brother, Tom, who suggested that he should come home for Christmas; he assured him they would take all necessary precautions, that he need have no fear. Tom recalled Christmas Eve at Barnagurraha under the Galtees:

> Darkness set in and no Liam. The old home was so strange without him. We were all trying to be happy at supper, I being the one to know he would surely attempt to come. How often I walked out into the darkness and listened sadly. At 8.30 a knock at the door, and rushing out to receive another rebel – Denny Hannigan, afterwards Brigade General of East Limerick – Liam was waiting behind the pier of the gate lest some of the neighbours' were in the house. At that time people had not learned to keep their tongues quiet. That was a great night. Three of us brothers watched the boreen, each his turn of an hour till dawn ... Nobody knew he was home that Christmas. After dark, each night, I strolled with him for hours down the old boreen and he was happy. He would talk on one subject only – The Irish Republic.

On 7 January 1920 he travelled to Dublin accompanied by Tadgh Crowley and Éamon Tobin. He remained there until 7 March, staying with the O'Mahony family, at De Courcy Square. During these two months he had continuous consultations with the staff of GHQ particularly with Richard Mulcahy and Michael Collins. He met Dan Breen and Seán Treacy; the group discussed plans for developing the fight; they had decided that there was no turning back at this point.

While in Dublin he had to undergo an operation for an undergrowth in a tooth. He was extremely anxious, as he feared that he might speak while under the anaesthetic. Consequently, he arranged for Dan Breen to be present during the operation. Happily Dan was able to assure him, afterwards, that he had said nothing.

One night he went to the theatre with Laurence O'Mahony, and Seán Treacy joined them. During the performance somebody sent word that the theatre might be raided. Instantly, they quietly left and had only reached O'Connell Street when the Abbey was surrounded. Fortunately the O'Mahony home was not under suspicion, so they were able to return there.

After some weeks Collins offered him the post of deputy chief-of-staff at headquarters. While he considered such an offer a great honour, nevertheless he weighed it up rather carefully; he didn't accept. In a letter to his mother he wrote, 'I intend remaining in the country to help the boys while things remain at their present pressure.' As a military man he preferred active service to an executive type of life, furthermore, he believed that he was needed in his own area as a military man. In a letter to his brother he conveyed his feelings, 'The Army has to hew the way to freedom for politics to follow.'

On 7 March he returned to Cork with some of his friends in the Tipperary hurling team, then travelled from the city to his own brigade area. Two weeks later, on 20 March 1920. Tomás Mac-Curtain, commandant of Cork No. 1 brigade and lord mayor of Cork was murdered by the RIC. Liam, with fellow officers, marched behind the remains. In a letter he wrote:

> You have heard, I expect, that I attended the Lord Mayor's funeral – yes, I and several like me risked anything and everything to see the last of a noble soldier. He was one of my best friends in the cause, and I have indeed felt terribly over him. He was foully murdered by the enemy, but the hour is at hand when they shall rue the moment they did so.[4]

In June 1919 Dáil Éireann had decreed the establishment in every county of national arbitration courts, as part of the general policy supplanting British institutions in Ireland. A police force, which would enforce the authority of these courts and enable them to function properly, was essential.

On the morning of 17 November 1919 two bank officials were travelling in a car from Millstreet to their branch offices in Knocknagree. One was carrying £10,000 and the other £6,700. Armed and masked men held them up at Ballydaly and robbed the total sum. The RIC, to whom the crime was reported, did very little to investigate it except to arrest a local volunteer who had absolutely no connection with the incident. The British stated that this action was carried out by members of Sinn Féin. Liam travelled to the Millstreet area to investigate the incident and, hopefully to bring the perpetrators to justice. The case was a difficult one; normal facilities which would be open to a police force were not at their disposal.

He got all local volunteer officers to work on whatever scraps of information were available but by mid-March 1920, they had had no success. Local officers were deeply impressed by his methods which finally led to the discovery of the criminals. The investigation involved a complete check of the population in the Ballydaly neighbourhood and the outcome led to the discovery of the money. This was proof of Liam's painstaking investigation.

On 24 April 1920 warrants were issued by the 'Republican police force' to arrest ten of the gang who had carried out the robbery. Eight of the wanted men were arrested. In order to carry out the arrests several houses were searched. The RIC in their fortified barracks, though no doubt aware of the position, did not dare interfere. Without jails, prisoners who had to be fed and guarded in the 'Republican' houses were a nuisance. Nevertheless, these prisoners were held in custody pending trial and Liam gave orders that they were to be treated as well as conditions permitted. This meant supplying them with tobacco and cigarettes. On 27 April, Liam himself presided over a special court, which tried the eight prisoners. At the second interrogation, preceding the court, the ring-leader confessed and disclosed the hiding place of his share of the money; four of his accomplices also confessed.

This meant that £9,208 had already been recovered before the court sitting. Seven of the prisoners were found guilty. Five were sentenced to deportation from Ireland for terms varying from fifteen years downwards and two were sentenced to exclusion from the brigade area. All the money recovered was returned to the bank.

Liam had demonstrated the integrity of the Republican army and its ability to detect and to punish wrong-doers. In turning aside from his principal duties in the volunteer force he had, by his action, raised the prestige of the whole organisation and set an example which put an effective end to similar acts of crime. His action not alone gained the approval of every law-abiding citizen but brought compliments from Michael Collins. In addition it had a wider significance – it showed the extent to which the RIC had abdicated its normal duties and were not concerned with the detection and punishment of perpetrators of crime or the protection of the community from criminal elements. Locals now began to place trust in the ability of Sinn Féin courts.

On 2 January 1920, Carrigtwohill barracks (after a fight in which the walls were breached by explosives) yielded arms and ammunition and on surrender the garrison was set free. It was the first barracks in Ireland to be captured since 1916. Many similar attacks began to take place all over Ireland. This resulted in the British authorities concentrating their forces in the larger towns and cities.

Because of widespread arrests, many IRA were forced to leave their places of normal employment and devote all their time to army duties. There were also widespread resignations from the RIC, which caused a crisis for the force and meant that the British government had to recruit other Englishmen. This, in turn, led to a new pseudo police force, the Auxiliary division. British procedure dictated that they did not admit the existence of war in Ireland, but instead maintained that they were dealing with gangs of criminals who terrorised the population. Sir Nevil Macready records discussions, which he had with Sir Henry Wilson, chief of the imperial general staff:

I was in absolute agreement on the understanding that the government would provide the necessary means to use 'a strong hand' in 'stamping out the rebellion'.[5]

The RIC had now ceased to perform the ordinary duties of a police force. With the armed Auxiliaries they actively opposed the IRA. Because of the ruthless policy many resigned, some joined the IRA, some remained in the force and worked as agents for the IRA. Attacks on police barracks became commonplace.

In 1920 the Black and Tans were brought to Ireland. Commissioner Smyth, appointed for Munster, visited Listowel barracks on 19 June 1920 and in a speech proclaiming his policies he said, 'I am getting 7,000 police from England. Police and military will patrol the country at least five nights a week. They are not to confine themselves to the main roads but to take across the country, to lie in ambush, and when civilians are seen approaching, shout, "Hands Up". Should the order not be immediately obeyed, shoot, and shoot with effect. If persons approaching carry their hands in their pockets and are in any way suspicious-looking shoot them down ... The more you shoot the better I will like it, and I assure you no policeman will get into trouble for shooting any man ... We want your assistance in carrying out this scheme and wiping out Sinn Féin.' Jeremiah Mee took off his uniform belt and arms, laid them on the table and said, 'By your accent I take it you are an Englishman and in your ignorance you forget you are addressing Irishmen.' Eighteen others left with him.[6]

This 'shoot with effect' was the type of action which Liam Lynch and members of the volunteer force had to face but they remained determined to overcome this challenge.

Arrested with Tomás MacCurtain

Dáil Éireann, the Irish Volunteers, Sinn Féin, Cumann na mBan and the Gaelic League were now prohibited. Military and police raids at all hours of day and night had become commonplace. The jails in Ireland were filling up.

General Sir Nevil Macready was appointed GOC to the British forces in Ireland on 23 March 1920 and took up duty on 14 April. Shortly afterwards, Sir Hamar Greenwood was appointed chief secretary. Macready had discussions with Sir Henry Wilson, chief of the imperial general staff. He records: 'Before I crossed to Dublin we had several long talks on the general situation, from which it was clear that he firmly held to a policy of stamping out rebellion with a strong hand, a policy with which I was in absolute agreement on the understanding that the government would provide the necessary means.' He proceeded to use a 'strong hand' and records that by the end of April 1920, 241 known or suspected IRA officers had been dealt with, and that a third of them came from County Cork.[1]

Lynch in Cork No. 2 brigade had built up the confidence of his volunteer group. Their morale was high and they had a binding element of brotherhood and unity. His letters during this period reflect his contentment. 'It's a grand generation to live in,' he wrote.[2] The decision to make a success of the struggle was coupled with determination to succeed against all odds. Liam, with the other men, had not taken the decision lightly. Large bodies of men had adjusted themselves mentally to a new concept of the historic struggle. They were prepared for self sacrifice, loyalty and daring. This national movement was different from all previous attempts to attain liberty. The guerrilla idea was a fundamental departure from previous policies, and military assistance from outside would be insignificant, except for the purchase of arms where possible. It was a national policy, recognised by their national government, constitutionally elected by the votes of an overwhelming majority of the people. Despite attack by the British forces there was no serious disruption of IRA activity.

In March 1920 when Liam returned to his brigade, he moved his headquarters from Glenville to a more central location, Mourne Abbey. Liam continued to give officers the maximum amount of authority and freedom of action, and then hold them responsible for the result. The development of guerrilla warfare was built on the amount of captured arms which each unit could secure. In May 1920 Liam was worried by inactivity in other areas and expressed official concern. 'Those places where guerilla warfare against the enemy has been waged with great activity and effectiveness represent only a small portion of the country. In some parts there has been marked inactivity. Officers who are neglecting their duty must get on or get out.'[3] Because of Liam's excellent organisation, his ability to make quick decisions and to use initiative helped him to play a competent part in the fight for freedom in Cork No. 2 brigade. Together with Cork No. 1 and Cork No. 3 brigades, Cork county played a large part (if not a major part) in gaining freedom for Ireland.

At Mourne Abbey stores, brigade headquarters, Liam was joined by Vice-commandant George Power, who was just beginning to take up full time active service. Power was now on the run; on 1 April he was arrested in his parents' home in Fermoy. Having asked permission from the officer in charge to go upstairs to collect some clothing, he went into a bedroom, locked the door and escaped through a window.

During this time, Michael Fitzgerald and his comrades remained in Cork jail. Liam drew up rescue plans on several occasions, but it was felt that possible casualties would be too great. Liam decided that if the British authorities could take officers of the IRA and put them in jail, the IRA should in turn capture British officers. His volunteer intelligence organisation reported that some of them fished on the Blackwater. Liam set 26 June as an attempted date of the kidnapping. He selected two officers, Seán Moylan and Patrick Clancy who would, with George Power and himself, capture the men.

A few days before the twenty-sixth Liam and George Power moved into the Fermoy battalion area, got safe hiding, made a final check on the details and finalised their plans. Moylan and Clancy were to travel in a car owned by Curtin of Newmarket. Five miles east of Fermoy, scouts were posted on Saturday morning to watch the fishing pool. They reported seeing General Lucas and his personal servant fishing with two other officers. Moylan, Clancy, Power and Lynch went to the fishing hut, arrested the general's personal servant, and set about rounding up the three British officers. Taken completely by surprise the first officer offered no resistance and he was led back a prisoner. Shortly afterwards a second officer was found and also captured. Coming through a small wood, George Power came face to face with Lucas and disarmed him. Lucas was marched back to the lodge. When the men assembled the prisoners in the fishing lodge, neither Liam nor his companions were aware of the identity of the two officers accompanying the general. When George Power gave Lucas the names and ranks of the IRA officers, he asked if he had any objection to doing likewise, he said he had none. Lucas pointed to Colonel Danford of the Royal Artillery and Colonel Tyrell of the Royal Engineers. 'You are to be held as prisoners,' Lynch said, 'until we get further instructions from headquarters. Meanwhile we will grant you facilities normally accorded prisoners such as you.'

Lucas' servant, upon release, was given a letter written by Lynch to the commanding officer of the British forces at Fermoy, notifying him of the capture of the three officers and stating that they would be treated as prisoners of war.

Volunteer Owen Curtin was the driver with Lucas and Lynch and Clancy accompanied Danford. Power and Seán Moylan took Tyrell, the other officer, in the Ford and they set out in the direction of Mourne Abbey. The arrangement was that both cars would if possible keep in touch, with the Ford travelling 50 to 100 yards ahead of the other car. For a time all went well.

In order to avoid passing through Fermoy the cars headed south. Just about two miles south of Rathcormac, the captured officers made a bid for freedom. Lucas and Danford held a brief conversation in Arabic and together they sprang on Lynch and Clancy. The sudden attack put them at a disadvantage, and because of the fight the driver lost control, crashed into the roadside ditch and became unconscious. The struggle between Liam Lynch and General Lucas was particularly severe, both being athletic and trained men. The door of the touring car gave way, and both men were thrown on the roadway and the struggle continued until finally Lynch overpowered Lucas. Meanwhile Danford and Clancy were fighting desperately on the roadside. Danford was getting the better of the encounter when Lynch, having overpowered Lucas, turned around and saw Clancy being choked. He shouted to Danford, 'Surrender or I'll shoot!' Danford ignored the command. Lynch fired. The bullet hit Danford on the face and he collapsed over his opponent.

Power and Moylan, with their prisoners, had gone ahead in the Ford and had not noticed that the other car was not following. When they noticed, they went back and found the touring car lying in the ditch with the driver unconscious at the wheel. On the grass verge nearby, Danford was lying in a pool of blood and General Lucas was bending over him giving him first aid. Liam was doing the same for Paddy Clancy. When the volunteer driver in the wrecked car regained consciousness, they decided that he should go to the nearby village of Rathcormac and get a doctor.

Meanwhile Lynch took Lucas and changed to the Ford car, they turned west near Rathcormac and on to Mourne Abbey. In the home of John O'Connell they left their captive and Lynch. O'Connell found the two men were of such reserved personalities that he 'did not even know captive from captor until the prisoner was put to bed.' Lynch instructed George Power to go to Dublin and inform Cathal Brugha and Michael Collins of current happenings.

That afternoon one of the members of the O'Connell family came home on holidays. He informed Lynch of reports circulating in the town that the British intended to carry out reprisals for the capture of General Lucas. Consequently Lynch dispatched a note via Michael McCarthy, stating that Lucas was being held as a prisoner of war and was being treated as such. This, however, did not save the town; for the second time the British carried out widespread destruction; shop windows were broken and there was large scale looting and much intimidation. Meanwhile, searches using aircraft and large forces of infantry and lorries continued over a wide area. Mrs O'Neill, the caretaker at the fishing lodge, was closely questioned but divulged nothing. In the hope that she would break down, her son, Patrick, was taken into custody; but neither, however, betrayed the volunteers.

The following night General Lucas was transferred to Lombardstown and afterwards to the West Limerick brigade area and from there to Michael Brennan O/C of the East Clare brigade. Lucas was accommodated in various houses in the Clare brigade area but because of widespread activity in the region, it was again necessary to transfer him into the Limerick district. He had been in custody over a month when, on 30 July 1920 as he was being transferred from East Clare to the mid Limerick brigade, he escaped from his escort near Oola and from there he got back to his own forces.

Following General Lucas' escape, he reported his impressions of the IRA to his forces in a document, which was later captured. He stated that he was impressed by their standard of discipline, determination and efficiency. It was his opinion that the British forces in Ireland were confronted with a much braver military situation than was generally realised; he also stated that he foresaw a bitter struggle and that it would be necessary to employ a much larger force at British army garrisons, if the IRA was to be defeated.

On the night of 12 August 1920 Lynch attended an IRB meeting in Cork. On the way to Cork he had told Patrick Mc-

Centre: *General Lucas*
Front row: *Paddy Brennan and Joe Keane*
Back row: *Paddy and Michael Brennan*
(Courtesy, Cork Public Museum)

Carthy who accompanied him, that he did not know the city very well but wanted to see Terence MacSwiney. At Dublin Hill outside the city, Lynch instructed McCarthy to go into the city and make an appointment with the Lord Mayor, Terence Mac-Swiney.[4] After some difficulty McCarthy saw MacSwiney and arranged a meeting between the two men at City Hall at 7 o'clock.

The British had raided some mail on 9 August and discovered that some officers were to meet in the City Hall three days later. A Dáil Éireann court for the city was in session in the council chambers when the British military swooped on them. Judges, lawyers, witnesses, prisoners and members of the general public were among the mixed group. The military raiding party surrounded the block of buildings including the City Hall, the Corporation Stores and Cornmarket to the rear of it. With a number of IRA officers Terence MacSwiney had succeeded in getting into the sheds at the back of the City Hall, but was discovered and placed under arrest. All were released with the exception of twelve, which included Liam Lynch and Terence Mac-Swiney.

As far as the British forces were concerned it was the most important capture of the war in Munster – almost the entire staff of the Cork No. 1 brigade and also some of the most active battalion commandants were taken in. All the prisoners, except Liam Lynch and Michael Leahy, gave correct names and addresses. Liam gave his name as James Casey and his address as 25 Camden Street, Dublin, according to the prison records. Michael Leahy gave his name as Thomas Power. Terence MacSwiney proposed to his fellow prisoners that they would go on hunger-strike. None of the men, including Liam Lynch, though not enthusiastic about using a hunger-strike as a weapon, expressed any disagreement with this proposal.

The prisoners were held at the Cork military detention barracks for one night and the next day they were removed to Cork jail. Here Liam met, for the last time, his old friend and comrade Michael Fitzgerald. His cousin, Tom Crawford was also in prison. Three days later on 15 August the British authorities released all of the prisoners (captured at City Hall) except Terence Mac-Swiney. He had a harrowing experience and died on 25 October after seventy-five days on hunger-strike.

Had the British authorities realised that they had Liam Lynch in their possession they certainly would not have released him. Two men of the same name were killed around this time. On the night of 4 August a man named James Lynch who was living in Hospital, Co. Limerick was questioned closely by three soldiers but no attempt was made to arrest him. The family knelt down to say the rosary but the soldiers, who had left, returned before the prayers were finished and beckoned to Lynch to go out as they wanted a word with him. He walked about 200 yards from his house when three volleys were fired and he fell dead.

On the night of 22 September 1920 a John Lynch from Kilmallock who was a county councillor and Gaelic League enthusiast was staying in the Exchange Hotel, Dublin. Two officers in British uniform went to his room and about an hour and a half after they had left, a party of police arrived. Later the body of

Councillor Lynch was found stretched across the bed. He had been shot at close range by a revolver carrying a silencer. The British authorities discovered that the wrong man had been shot, and in an effort to hush up the murder it was officially announced that no inquest would be permitted and a public funeral would not be allowed. Three separate reports differing in essential points were issued. It was alleged that Councillor Lynch had fired on the crown forces while being arrested and had to be shot in self-defence; but independent doctors stated that he had been shot at close range and that there was no sign of a struggle.

On the night of 15 August when Liam Lynch was released from Cork jail he stayed in the Cork area in the home of Joe O'Connor. Despite the fact that he had been on hunger-strike for four days and was possibly a little weak he was extremely anxious to get back to his own battalion area. When he arrived, he discovered that Patrick Clancy, who had taken part in the Lucas raid, had been killed when the local flying column attacked a British military plane. Following his jail ordeal and news that the authorities hoped to eliminate an IRA member named Lynch, he became even more determined to recruit full-time members for the flying column.

Terence MacSwiney with his wife Muriel and daughter Máire. The photograph was taken around the time of his arrest in 1920 prior to his hunger strike
(Courtesy, Cork Public Museum)

Hostilities intensify – death of a true friend

In mid-1920 the British army of occupation in Ireland exceeded in strength the first British expeditionary forces sent to France to fight the Germans in 1914. At this time in Ireland the British army were experiencing difficulty in combating guerrilla warfare.

Liam Lynch set about organising a two weeks' training course for the volunteers of No. 2 brigade. He outlined to his staff and members of the brigade column his intention of creating an active service unit in each battalion so that a column of eighteen to thirty men could, with the available arms, be capable of combined action for larger operations. At the conclusion of the training course, battalion officers with the column would return to their own commands.

Lynch next planned the capture of the barracks at Mallow, which was housed by the Seventeenth Lancers. At the time two volunteers, Richard Willis and John Bolster, were employed on the maintenance staff, so they kept an eye on their routine movements. The garrison consisted of non-commissioned officers and men, and an officer who normally left the barracks each morning to exercise the horses. From the reports by Willis and Bolster, Lynch and his staff were able to draw up sketch maps of the barracks.

Owen Harold, who had been billeted in a house facing the barracks helped by giving details of the troops' movements. As the barracks was situated in a narrow street it was difficult for the volunteers to carry out the attack, but they assembled under cover of darkness in the nearby town hall the night before the attack was to take place. On 28 September 1920 Bolster and Willis arrived for work at the usual time, bringing Patrick McCarthy with them as a contractor's overseer. McCarthy was to hold up the guardroom when the attacking party arrived at the gate. McCarthy, Willis and Bolster were armed with revolvers.

The routine garrison left at the usual time and the 'contractor's overseer' went through the routine of measuring the doors and windows while he waited for his comrades outside to begin the operation. At around 9.30 a.m. Ernie O'Malley knocked on the door beside the main gate. When the sentry pushed back the slide over the peephole O'Malley pushed in an envelope saying, 'this is for the barrack warden'. The sentry had to open the door in order to take the envelope but O'Malley said that he would personally like to give it to the barrack warden. The sentry hesitated at this unusual request giving O'Malley the opportunity of moving closer to him; he grabbed the sentry's rifle and wrestled it out of his hands. Paddy O'Brien and another volunteer, immediately behind O'Malley, pushed the door open. Liam Lynch and a small party were on their heels. They made for the guardroom, which was situated about thirty yards from the entrance gate and midway in the block of buildings. On the pretext of examining some defects, McCarthy, Willis and Bolster had been waiting beside the guardroom. They rushed into the room and held up the guard. Inside the main entrance there was an open shed where the senior NCO, Sergeant Gibbs, was supervising the showing of a horse. When he saw the first man of the raiding party he rushed towards the guardroom. One of the volunteers ordered him to halt. He ignored the order and a shot was fired over his head, but still he did not stop. A bullet hit him leaving him mortally wounded at the door. The rest of the people in the guardroom were then marched out on to the square and held there until the remainder of the garrison was collected. First aid was given, under supervision, to the wounded sergeant; the remainder was locked into one of the stables. While this was happening Lynch had given the pre-arranged signal to the three waiting cars which were driven into the yard; all the arms, ammunition and useful equipment was piled into them. (The arms consisted of two Hotchkiss light machine-guns, 27 rifles, a revolver, very light pistols, 4,000 rounds of ammunition and a quantity of bayonets and lances.) They set the stores on fire and intended to burn the entire building, but shortly after the volunteers left, the fire was put out.

When they left the barracks each man carried a rifle and two bandoleers of ammunition. The operation was carried out with speed. The drivers of the three cars, Leo O'Callaghan, Seán and Paddy Healy, took the road to Glashbee where the Ahadillane company took over local protection of the material for the night. All the members of the raiding party moved back to base without any casualties, and the captured arms were later distributed among the men. Lynch had instructed his men before the attack that shots should be fired only when absolutely necessary. Though he regretted the casualty, he was jubilant at the results of the highly successful first action of the flying column. It was the first occasion in Ireland in which an enemy military post was captured and stripped of its arms and equipment in daylight. Willis and Bolster, who joined the column, were trained to operate and maintain the two captured machine-guns by volunteer Matt Flood of Fermoy who had served as a machine-gunner in the British army.

After the raid, the civilian population of Mallow were harassed; looting and harassment was indiscriminately carried out. Several members of the British forces from Mallow, Buttevant and Fermoy set about burning and looting public and private property in Mallow. The town hall and local creamery were burned; drunken troops roamed the streets, indiscriminately throwing petrol-filled bottles, smashing windows and causing general havoc in the town.

Eight months after this event on 23 May 1921 a number of men who had been arrested were court-martialled at Victoria barracks in Cork. Six men, none of whom took part in the raid, were charged with the murder of Sergeant Gibbs; five were sentenced to death and, of the five, one was not a volunteer. Liam Lynch made a public statement in connection with the affair:

> As the officer in charge of the operation in question I desire to state publicly that none of these men had any part in it. Furthermore, I wish to state that I alone am responsible for all that was done on that occasion. The raid on the barracks was carried out as

a military operation on my orders by a body of Republican troops acting under my direction and I acted by virtue of my commission as an officer of the Irish Republican Army under the authority of my superior officer and the government of the Irish Republic, in accordance with the law of regular warfare.

Signed Liam Ó Loingsigh O/C Cork No. 2 Brigade[1]

Lynch in a further statement published in 16 July issue of *An tÓglach*, stated that Denis Buckley, Farran, Mourne Abbey, who had also been sentenced to death was not a member of the IRA and had nothing whatever to do with the attack. However, none of those court-martialled was actually put to death.

Following the capture of Mallow barracks the column that had billeted in Lombardstown moved to Ardglass in the Charleville battalion area on 30 September. An attack on Churchtown RIC barracks was called off when it was discovered that the post was aware of the plan. The flying column then moved to Freemount where they contacted officers of the Drumcollogher battalion of West Limerick. Patrick O'Brien of Liscarroll was appointed column commander.

Seán Moylan came to Lynch with a proposal for an attack on a military party which travelled at least once a week by lorry between Kanturk and Newmarket. The towns, four miles apart, had strong garrisons of military and police. Lynch, O'Malley and Moylan inspected the position and while doing so saw two lorries containing twenty-four British soldiers pass.

At approximately 3 a.m. on 6 October, the column moved across the fields to occupy the position at Ballygrochane. Shortly after 11 a.m. they heard the long-awaited sound of the lorry. As two lorries were expected, Lynch had planned to let the first one well into position before the four men made a road-block with a cart. When signalled into action these men pushed the cart out and ran for cover. The lorry stopped and as there was only one vehicle, the elaborate preparations were unnecessary. The fight was over in five minutes. The driver was killed and the remainder of the party wounded. The column had no casualties. Lynch felt that this ambush was successful from two points of view. Apart from the amount of arms collected, it also gave experience to large numbers of men. Lynch then set about mobilising large contingents of the Kanturk and Newmarket battalions and employed them on protective duties.

Because of what had happened at Mallow, Lynch decided that the British forces would not find the civilian population of Kanturk without defence should reprisals be carried out. He marched his column to occupy Kanturk; a local company in the town had been watching activities and units were posted to cover the creamery and the main business areas of the town, but there were no reprisals that night. The column withdrew at dawn. The British forces made some surprise swoops later; Clancy and O'Connell who had been trapped and had tried to resist arrest were killed. Despite the risks involved Lynch attended their funerals in Kanturk. As an added protection from this period onwards Liam 'ordered' that all men who feared that they might be arrested at any time should be permanently armed. The brigade column was demobilised at the end of October and from then on each battalion began to build up its own column of fifteen to thirty men, they were to bear in mind the possibility of combining forces, if at any time they were confronted with a large operation.

The railway system, throughout this period, was invaluable to the IRA. It was a reliable method of maintaining contact between brigade areas and between Fermoy brigade headquarters and GHQ. Generally it took only two days for a dispatch to travel from the Fermoy area to GHQ. The employees involved with the volunteers were extremely well organised and efficient. From both Mallow and Fermoy a service of cyclist dispatch riders travelled between battalion headquarters and adjoining brigades; working in relays these dispatch riders operated day and night from company to company. The use of bicycles was prohibited except under permit from the British forces so very often horse-drawn transport was used. In the Fermoy area the British forces used a type of cavalry service and often searched those who were carrying dispatches, thus creating further problems for the volunteers.

On 9 August 1920 the Restoration of Order in Ireland Act became law. This meant, from the British point of view, that they had now legalised terror in Ireland. Court-martials and military courts could now try persons for treason, felony and lesser offences, uncontrolled powers of arrest and internment were placed in the hands of military authorities and trials under the act could be held in secret. The turn which events were taking troubled Liam. In a letter to Fr Tom he expressed his concern for the fate of his imprisoned comrades. Michael Fitzgerald imprisoned since September 1919 with a number of other untried prisoners in Cork gaol went on hunger-strike in August 1920.[2] Liam and Michael Fitzgerald were extremely good friends. Liam was worried about him but felt it would be impossible for the British to procure any evidence connecting Fitzgerald with the Fermoy raid of September 1919. However, Fitzgerald was a determined man and continued with his hunger-strike for sixty-seven days. He died on 17 October 1920, and brought sadness to all his comrades. His body was taken to the mortuary at Fermoy church. The night before his burial Liam came in and had the coffin lid removed to look for the last time on the face of the man to whom he was most deeply attached – his best friend was gone. His funeral took place from SS Peter and Paul's church in Cork.

After the Mass, British soldiers wearing steel helmets and carrying fixed bayonets, invaded the church and walked over the seats to the altar rails. With a drawn revolver, an officer handed a notice to the priest stating that only a limited number of persons would be allowed to take part in the funeral. A machine-gun was mounted at the church gates and armoured cars toured the vicinity. Yet despite this, thousands took part in the funeral procession while armoured cars and tenders carrying heavily equipped forces accompanied the cortège to the city boundary.

Fermoy witnessed similar scenes the following day when Fitzgerald was buried at Kilcrumper. Some hours after the grave had been closed many of his comrades assembled to pay their last tribute to a heroic soldier. Again Liam risked his life and returned to pay his respects to his friend. Amid the strains under which Liam worked during the following years he never forgot Michael Fitzgerald. Indeed, when his own hour came to die, his last request was to be buried beside his old comrade at Kilcrumper.

Seán O'Brien, Charleville, chairman Rural District Council, supporter of the Gaelic League and Sinn Féin (not an IRA member) killed by Black and Tans in front of his wife and four year old daughter (Courtesy, Michael McGrath & Peter Somers)

IRA guard of honour at the funeral of Seán O'Brien. L/R: Jack White, Michael Ryan, Jim Quirke, Johnny White, Mick Shine, Michael Geary (Courtesy, Michael McGrath & Peter Somers)

More comrades shot

In November 1920 a group of British intelligence men, known as the Cairo Gang posed as businessmen and lodged in various houses in Dublin. Through his intelligence operations, their activities became known to Michael Collins. In simultaneous pre-dawn raids on Sunday 21 November Michael Collins' squad killed eleven British intelligence officers. In retaliation the Black and Tans invaded the football match at Croke Park that afternoon and fired indiscriminately at the teams and at an estimated seven thousand spectators, killing twelve civilians including one of the Tipperary players and wounding sixty.

In Millstreet, County Cork, the RIC, the Macroom based Auxiliaries and the Black and Tans had subjected the citizens to a wild night of firing. Because of the way the RIC Auxiliary patrol was attacking civilians, some members of a small battalion column took up positions on the night of 22 November and, in the fight which ensued, two Black and Tans were wounded. The brigade suffered a serious blow, Captain Patrick McCarthy, who had joined the volunteers immediately after 1916, was killed.[1] On the night of his death he was attended by Fr Joe Breene and later that night his body was removed to Eugene O'Sullivan's house where it was guarded by his comrades. The next night, Liam took charge of the funeral procession to Lismire where he was buried with full military honours. Anticipating British reprisals for the shooting of the Black and Tans, the IRA occupied Millstreet in order to protect its inhabitants. However, the British did not leave their post, so before dawn he sent the column to billets outside the town.

At Kilmichael outside Macroom, on Sunday, 28 November 1920, thirty-six volunteers of the Third West Cork flying column, under the command of Tom Barry, successfully carried out the first major guerrilla ambush against the British forces in Ireland. During the ambush Barry's volunteers accepted in good faith a surrender call by the Auxiliaries. But the Auxiliaries resumed the fight and fatally wounded three of the volunteers. Barry and his men retaliated. Sixteen Auxiliaries (based in Macroom Castle) were killed in the ambush, another was seriously wounded and a further soldier was killed subsequently.[2] Large quantities of arms, ammunition and documents were secured.

Following this, Lord French announced 'Martial Law in the County of Cork, East and West Riding, the City of Cork, Tipperary, North and South Riding, the City and County of Limerick.'

Further to this General Sir Nevil Macready, commander-in-chief of British forces in Ireland, proclaimed that persons caught with illegal arms or explosives were liable to sentence of death. Public meetings were forbidden and each householder was to affix a list of the occupants inside his/her front door. Indiscriminate shooting of people pursuing their ordinary peaceful activities was the order of the day as was the burning of shops, creameries and other stores.

A notice printed in all the daily newspapers and displayed in Macroom 'ordered that all males passing through Macroom shall not appear in public with their hands in their pockets. Any male infringing this order is liable to be shot at sight'.

(Outside Mitchelstown in Lynch's area one evening in July 1920, a group of boys and girls were having a crossroads dance when a military lorry passed by and opened fire. Amidst a hale of bullets, the boys and girls ran for shelter. Two men, McDonnell and McGrath had been shot dead and the military immediately left. Subsequently, at an inquest, the soldiers swore that they were attacked and had fired in self-defence. The jury, despite British intimidation, brought in a verdict of murder against the soldiers.)

Liam Lynch continued to take every opportunity, which presented itself in each of his seven battalion areas, to attack British forces. On 19 December a successful ambush was fought under the command of Thomas Barry at Glencurrane near Liam's birthplace. The columns captured eighteen rifles, five or six hundred rounds of ammunition and two dozen mills grenades. Of the eighteen men in the two lorries, two had been killed and three wounded. The Fermoy column, under the command of Patrick Egan, surprised a lorry of British troops near Castlelyons. The first volley that they fired hit the driver. The lorry crashed and its occupants scattered through the fields and were pursued by the IRA who forced nine British soldiers to surrender their arms.

At the beginning of 1920 Liam's brigade had had very few arms but by July quite a substantial amount of serviceable rifles, revolvers and grenades had been acquired. Most of the arms and equipment had been captured from the occupation forces, and Liam was completely aware that they had to depend on their own resources, so they would have to continue to capture more arms in order to maintain the struggle. At the beginning of 1920 only a few members of the brigade were on whole-time active service, but by the end of the year, seven columns, each varying in strength from fourteen to thirty men were in the field, all able to get reinforcements from their own battalions at short notice.

Another colleague of Liam's, Liam O'Connell, was shot in an attack on an armoured car in Dublin on 14 October 1920. When he was being buried at Glantane, near Mallow, Liam made one of his brief public statements:

> We are here at the grave of one of our volunteers whose young life is given for the freedom of Ireland. We will revenge his great sacrifice and will continue the fight until it is brought to a successful conclusion. Many more may follow Liam O'Connell before this country obtains its Independence.

The deaths of young officers like McCarthy, Clancy, O'Connell and Michael Fitzgerald were all severe blows to the brigade, yet the deaths of these young men somehow strengthened the hearts of their comrades; it heightened their morale and gave them the strength and determination to fight on. Liam mentioned this in a letter to his mother:

I am living only to bring the dreams of my dead comrades to reality and every moment of my life is now devoted to that end ... Thank God I am left alive to still help in shattering the damned British Empire.[3]

Tom Barry

Intelligence

Throughout the long struggle of Irish history previous armed efforts to achieve liberty had often been weakened and sometimes frustrated by the activities of spies and informers. Some RIC members, since its establishment, had faithfully passed on information to Britain. Its countrywide stations were manned by a body of men generally conscientious and intelligent in the discharge of their duties; they had unrivalled knowledge of the inhabitants of their area, which meant that there was a constant flow of information to Dublin Castle.

The RIC was not now receiving any new recruits, indeed many of those in the force had resigned because of an order from GHQ –'Volunteers shall have no intercourse with the RIC and shall stimulate and support in every way the boycott of this force by the Dáil.'[1] This was a shattering blow to the mainstay of British espionage in Ireland, so soldiers were sent into the country pretending to be deserters. 'Stool Pigeons' were put into jails and internment camps where they could gather information. Also Britain's own loyal supporters throughout the country had eyes and ears for any activity carried on by the IRA and constantly sought information on IRA activities.

The IRA, on the other hand, built up an intelligence organisation with the help of local people that with time, proved highly efficient. The IRA intelligence unit was extremely effective, with agents in each army unit and an espionage service inside British organisations wherever possible. At GHQ, the director of intelligence, Michael Collins had his own extremely well organised force. But Collins would have been powerless outside Dublin, were it not for the work done by the local brigades.

Early in 1920 Liam appointed brigade and battalion intelligence officers. Numbers of men in sections varied according to local needs; the principal duties entailed the security of their own forces and the gathering of maximum information on organisation, strength, tactics, together with routine and intentions of British garrisons in each town and district. The company section reported, through the company captain, to the battalion intelligence officer whose duty it was to assemble and co-ordinate these reports and then send to the brigade everything of significance.

Some who worked in post offices or in any British organisation kept regular contact with the IRA and made arrangements for the regular transmission of dispatches and documents. Since early 1917 Siobhán Creedon, who had worked in Mallow post office, had secured valuable information. She supplied Liam Lynch and George Power, at brigade headquarters in Creedon's house, with a carbon copy of all messages of interest. Siobhán was to lose her job when an enquiry was undertaken, because it was discovered that she had made an extra carbon copy for the IRA.[2]

She had secured valuable information with regard to British plans for conscription in 1919 and these were transmitted to Richard Mulcahy, chief-of-staff. Since early 1920 almost all the post offices in the brigade area were included in the intelligence network and this was of the greatest value to the brigade as the telegraph and telephone systems were used extensively by the RIC. Very often urgent messages were sent over the wire in cipher copies. The IRA intelligence system working within the post offices, copied these messages, and transmitted them to the intelligence officers who then deciphered them from a key supplied by the director of intelligence.

In Lynch's area, a British officer from the Fermoy garrison, Lieut Vincent, disguised as a tramp, was captured in Watergrasshill. When searched by the IRA he was found to be in possession of a notebook containing a list of names of persons known to be loyal to the British. The IRA had known of the garrison's activities but now they had proof. On the morning following his capture there was a big round up by the British forces and Lieut Vincent was mortally wounded when he attempted to escape.

Many deserters from the British army started to come to local officers saying they wanted to join the IRA. Some of them were genuine deserters but others were engaged in spying. Where it was found, following a court marital, that men were not genuine deserters, some were executed and pseudo-deserters stopped approaching the IRA.

Regular exchange of information took place between the three Cork brigades, all of whom liaised with Michael Collins, director of intelligence. Valuable material was sent to Collins in Dublin from brigades throughout the country but particularly from County Cork. According to Florence O'Donoghue, 'There were cases in which communications issued by Major General Strickland did not reach his brigade commanders more than a day before they were in the hands of the IRA brigade commanders opposing them.'[3]

Spies

On 12 January 1921 a proclamation was issued which prohibited the use of motor cars, motor cycles or pedal cycles between 8 p.m. and 6 a.m. A copy of the military governor's proclamation was torn down in Fermoy on Liam Lynch's instructions. The town was subsequently fined £100. As the fine remained unpaid, crown forces collected it in kind from four traders in the form of wines and spirits. The *Daily Express* on 4 January commented: 'This is, of course, Martial Law. It is legal and disciplined. It is, we must believe, necessary. But it is horrible'.

A member of the volunteer forces, carrying arms when captured, could now be tried by drumhead court-martials and executed forthwith. Under this martial law the first official execution which took place was that of an officer of Liam Lynch's brigade – Cornelius Murphy, one of the founder members of Millstreet battalion column. On 4 January, he went home to visit his parents in Kerry and was captured. He was taken to Cork military barracks, court-martialled on a charge of being in possession of a loaded revolver, and sentenced to death. He was shot on 1 February 1921.

Towards the end of January 1921 Lynch accompanied by some volunteers lay in wait for the Auxiliaries west of Newmarket. 'Four lorries passed, but we had to let them go,' said Paddy O'Brien, 'because they had civilian hostages – this was part of the tactics which they used to foil our efforts.'

Next day the men waited from 6 a.m. until well after dark beside a dugout. 'There was a thick wet fog, and the cold was penetrating.' The following morning they again took up positions at 6 a.m. 'This was a cold dry day. It was going to be a fight to the finish, Liam told us. It had to be because we were in a difficult ambush position, without any hope of retreat. Liam emphasised, it was we who were taking them on, and we had the advantage like Tom Barry at Kilmichael,' Paddy O'Brien recalls. (Paddy O'Brien,

Liscarroll was Tom Barry's first cousin.)

About midday two cars were sighted approaching from the west. The first car skidded to a halt when the driver saw the trench. The second pulled up behind it. The ambush party opened fire. The occupants of the cars took shelter behind a fence. After some fighting, Lynch blew the whistle and called upon the military to surrender. Their reply was a further volley of fire, so the fight resumed until two of their party had been killed, and practically every one of them was wounded. Then they surrendered. The arms captured were all collected, loaded into one of the cars and driven away. Lynch had taken the precaution of having volunteers detailed to fell some partially sawn trees so that the road could be blocked. As a decoy the volunteers had also felled trees on other routes. Consequently the search party which scoured the area after the ambush were frustrated in their efforts.

Comdt Paddy O'Brien, Liscarroll, Cork No. 2 brigade – close friend of Liam Lynch
(Courtesy, Michael McGrath & Peter Somers)

The Millstreet battalion under C. J. Meaney had been studying the possibility of launching an attack on British troops using a train passing through the area. From mid-January various plans were tried but somehow never achieved fruition. Lynch decided to move into the area for further investigation. Trains travelling east and west were both potential targets and a position near Drishanebeg was selected. One evening, on 11 February at 6.30 p.m. as darkness approached, the column went into position. Plans had been made to bring this train to a halt. A volunteer was detailed to travel on the train, inspect it and signal at a point in Rathcoole where two armed men were waiting. At the signal the volunteers boarded the train as it was leaving the station and approached the driver compelling him to stop. In the darkness, a lighted bicycle lamp placed on the track indicated the exact position at which the engine should halt. At this spot the whistle was blown and the military in the train were called on to surrender; they answered with a rifle shot. Fire was opened upon the carriages containing the military party and continued for about fifteen minutes. The British party then surrendered; one had been killed and practically all were wounded. The column collected fifteen rifles and 700 rounds of ammunition. They had no casualties.

Lynch's brigade suffered a reverse at Mourne Abbey on 15 February 1921. From information received, British officers were to hold a conference in the martial law area of Cork. On Sunday, 13 February Lynch assembled his men to occupy positions on the Fermoy/Cork road and the Mallow/Cork road with the intention of attacking a convoy going or returning from the conference. The usual signalling scouts and protective elements were posted and preparations were completed in the early hours of the morning of 15 February.

That morning, Siobhán Creedon, the intelligence agent, while cycling to Mallow, met two lorries of troops and police. When she reached Mallow she reported what she had seen to Daniel McDonnell of the Mallow company. McDonnell immediately cycled along the main road to Mourne Abbey and located Tadgh Byrne near the southern end of the ambush position. He gave him the information and together they crossed a stream flowing parallel to the road where Jack Cunningham and the riflemen were hidden. Then they heard the sound of gunfire. The protective section had been engaged. The shooting had started not on the main road but north-east of the ambuscade. The column suddenly found itself in the role of ambushed rather than ambusher. The British forces were equipped with machine-guns and adequate transport; therefore, those who could, withdrew. Three volunteers were killed and one who was badly wounded, subsequently died. Eight IRA men were captured, two of whom were later executed in Cork after trial by court-martial. It was the first time that one of Lynch's columns was caught unaware and it appeared as if an informer had been at work. The volunteers became very uneasy.

Up to now Lynch had had no great problem of this nature within his brigade but it did appear, on this occasion, that accurate information had been passed on to the enemy. They not only knew the time, but the place and plan of the ambush. He immediately put his intelligence men to work; it took nearly a month (when a similar less disastrous event occurred) to discover how the information was being passed to the enemy. One of the pseudo-deserters, whom the volunteers had trusted, was found to be the culprit. He was dealt with accordingly.

All through the months of January, February and March 1921 there were several sniping attacks throughout the Second Cork brigade area and British forces were unable to stop them. The IRA battalions continued to harass wherever possible and during that period lost only a few men and no arms.

An extremely long and arduous ambush took place under Lynch's command at Clonbainin between Kanturk and Mill-street on 3 March 1921, where Seán Moylan of Newmarket joined with Kerry No. 2 brigade under Commandant Tom McEllis-trim, and a detachment from Charleville under Paddy O'Brien. At approximately 10 a.m. three military lorries passed unattacked because the mine failed to explode. Shortly after 2 p.m. three more lorries came into view. Fire was opened on the leading lorry. The ambush continued for some hours. In this engagement they collected quite an amount of ammunition and suffered no casualties. British casualties were thirteen killed and fifteen wounded. Because of British activity in Lombardstown, Lynch was forced to move brigade headquarters further west to Nadd.

On a raw, foggy March morning under driving rain, the British forces staged one of their elaborate and well-planned efforts to annihilate the brigade staff and the columns in the Cork No. 2 area. Forces were drawn from Cork, Ballincollig, Buttevant, Fermoy and Kanturk. Before midnight on 9 March the British forces in armoured vehicles had been moving out and were armed with rifles, machine-guns, mortars and grenades. They had intended to make a swoop and to converge on the IRA. It was a well-planned and efficiently carried-out operation but its success was limited because of Lynch's prompt action on an intelligence report received earlier.

Earlier in the day on 9 March 1921 Judy O'Riordan of Buttevant passed on information of large-scale raiding in the Banteer direction. Lynch ordered the Charleville battalion out on a road-blocking task at certain specified points. This saved the Nadd column, which was in training, from a major disaster. Lynch had also sent dispatches to the Buttevant, Mallow and various other companies requesting them to engage in road-trenching, which completely upset the British forces. Several cars skidded and the British operation was unsuccessful.

Lynch, with Power and a number of men, went that same morning to Nadd Cross with the intention of attacking some passing lorries. The British detachment which came to Nadd Cross turned west, evidently with the intention of approaching their objective from the south. Units of the column in the scattered farmhouses were alerted. They, and the brigade officers, began to move westwards across the mountain. At one point unobserved British troops infiltrated the position and reached David Herlihy's house where some men were sleeping. They rushed into the house, hustled the half-dressed occupants out, shouting, 'We'll give you some of your own stuff now!' They lined the men up in a field and the officer said, 'When I say run ... run!' Morgan and Moloney made a dash for liberty and, though wounded, managed to get away. Three other men, Waters, Kiely and Herlihy were shot and then bayoneted to death.

The British forces, who had now been combing the entire area, were closing in on the volunteers. Fire was exchanged between some detachments and groups of volunteers. That evening Liam was informed that four were dead, including an unarmed civilian who was fired on and mortally wounded. Due to this and other circumstances it seemed to Liam that again his enemies were in possession of accurate information as to the volunteers' movements. There was a striking similarity between what had happened at Mourne Abbey and what had now taken place at Nadd. The mystery was finally cleared up. A member of the Kanturk column who had aroused his companions' suspicions was absent from Nadd during the attack. (He had served in the British army and had been with the column about two months.) Enquiries revealed that this man had known of the proposed ambush at Mourne Abbey several days before it was due to take place, likewise the Nadd raid. Two days before the Nadd raid he had said that he wanted to go to Kanturk to draw his British ex-service pension. Reflecting on the ambushes, which had taken place, the men realised that he had absented himself on each occasion that the military appeared to have been forewarned. Intelligence officer, Michael Moore warned the local men to watch this man's movements.

One night after drinking he was seen entering the British barracks where he remained for quite a while. Moore sent the information by dispatch to Liam, but for some reason, which is unclear, Liam never received this message. However, the man's guilt was confirmed when he was identified amongst the raiding group at Nadd dressed in the uniform of a Black and Tan. He was not seen again.[1]

Formation of First Southern Division

Liam Lynch continued to move with zeal through the seven battalion areas encouraging his men and perfecting the special skills which served the needs of the fighting column. He constantly replaced men who had been either arrested or killed. Movement through areas was extremely difficult as no house was entirely safe because of the sudden raids; no road was immune from cycle patrols or other army vehicles. Yet in the face of that situation Liam and his staff continued to move about in every part of the brigade area, if not freely, at least without any disruption of their duties. During all this time, since September 1919, he had never gone unarmed except on trips to Dublin or Cork. All his officers were permanently armed. They were also under orders to resist capture and avoid risks since August 1920.

Before billeting in any house Liam would inspect the layout, check any security arrangements and what action should be taken in the event of an attack, always detailing scouts to guard the house. During the early days he travelled by bicycle but later found it necessary to travel by pony and trap accompanied by at least one officer. The terrain of his brigade area posed difficulties as it was cut in two from west to east by the Blackwater, often restricting movement and causing delays. Coupled with this was the additional danger they had of crossing bridges. To overcome this difficulty boats were used mainly under cover of darkness. When the British forces discovered this method of transport they destroyed many boats.

On numerous occasions Liam escaped death or capture by the narrowest of margins, despite all precautions. Indeed, were he faced with capture, it probably would have been death, as he frequently stated, 'if I'm taken I'll never be taken alive.' Paddy O'Brien gives an example of one such occasion, which was on 18 March 1921 when George Power, Michael O'Connell, Maurice Walshe, Liam and O'Brien were moving on foot in daylight.

They were going up the mountain when they realised that the entire area was swarming with British troops who were engaged in a large scale combing operation. Liam and O'Brien were crawling ahead when Walshe caught up with them. 'The three of us sheltered under the merest cover near the top. It was the closest I've ever been to looking up the barrel of a gun. God! I can still feel that moment,' Paddy O'Brien recalls. The men remained motionless and were unobserved.

Liam's life was by this time an endless labour of planning and movement. Taking an overview of the inactive brigades he felt they should no longer remain dormant, because the British forces concentrated on the areas which were most active, and in fact at that time they had started to shift the weight of the occupation forces into Munster, and especially into the three Cork brigade areas. Liam felt that if this trend continued it could mean that the few active brigades might become more pressurised which in turn could have serious consequences for the entire movement. Though he realised that it was the responsibility of GHQ he nevertheless, by the end of 1920, consulted officers of the brigades directly adjoining his own. He wanted the flying columns to be organised into a type of army spirit and decided that this would necessitate co-ordination of the activities of the fighting forces in the south. The organisation, which had originally been quite small, was rapidly growing. A new situation was developing in the south and only in the south. The day of attacks on barracks was over. The struggle was developing into larger actions that required new tactics.

Because there were now greater dangers, new machinery was required. Liam's most frequent contacts were with Cork No. 1 and Tipperary No. 3 brigades, which bordered his own area. Dan Breen, Seán Treacy and Denis Lacey visited him a number of times. A visit by Dan Breen towards the end of 1920, resulted in an informal conference. This informal meeting to discuss the general situation was held near Bweening, eight miles from Mallow. Seán O'Hegarty and a member of the Cork No. 1 brigade,

Liam Deasy from Cork No. 3, and Liam himself with George Power from Cork No. 2 brigade attended. This resulted in the first formal conference of officers of the southern brigade which met at William Barry's, Glanworth, on 6 January 1921. Visiting officers from outside brigades were the guests of Liam Lynch's brigade. Though entirely loyal to HQ they realised that Dublin was far removed from the struggle in the south. They sent their recommendations and a summary of their decision to GHQ.[1]

In discussions which lasted two days and which were presided over by Séamus Robinson of Tipperary, with Con Moloney acting as adjutant, all the eleven officers present reviewed the factors influencing the struggle in their area. The consensus was that the war could be maintained and extended, coupled with a broad general agreement on the line of action to be undertaken. Seven of the fifteen companies of the Auxiliary division, each about a hundred strong, were stationed in the martial law area; British forces had been reinforced with armoured cars, which made movement very difficult for the volunteers. They had no heavy weapons for effective attacks and it was now almost impossible to raid any barracks as these were very heavily fortified. However, the morale of the IRA was high and, often because of the brutality meted out to civilians by the British forces, the people had become more supportive through a common bond.

At the conference, it was recommended that GHQ should openly state that the Republican army was on active service; that a proclamation should be issued to the effect that, where hostages were carried by the enemy, their forces armed or unarmed would be shot on sight; that in view of the British proclamation announcing that IRA men taken prisoners under arms would be shot forthwith, similar action would be taken by the IRA. The services of full-time medical officers would be sought and these should be paid for by headquarters. The most important recommendations suggested:

> to offer GHQ (a) an unarmed flying column of 20 men for each two brigades, i.e. these flying columns to be armed by GHQ and

sent by them to inactive areas; or (b) that the six brigades represented between them arm one flying column for similar action. GHQ to see to their quartering and rationing. It is suggested that this column operate in inactive areas and as far as possible from enemy active bases.[2]

This recommendation indicates how aware the assembled officers were of the necessity to spread the fight. Though short of arms they were nevertheless prepared to arm a column of twenty men out of their own resources so that the fight could be carried on in inactive areas.

From this period onwards arrangements were made for a more rapid exchange of intelligence between the brigades. It was decided to snipe at all enemy posts on one night each week and fire at them constantly by day. The key factor to emerge from the conference was that there should be mutual assistance between the brigades. The movement was also to become more widespread and take in the entire nation. This was the germ of a development for a divisional organisation initiated by Liam Lynch.

A second conference of the southern brigades was held at Hickey's in Glenville on 28 March 1921. This meeting included the representatives who had attended the previous meeting and also those of two Waterford and mid-Limerick brigades. The Third Cork and Second Cork brigades were represented by a larger group of officers who were involved with Donal Hales of Italy and Michael Collins in the importation of a cargo of arms from Italy. At the conference it was planned to get the arms shipment into Quince Harbour near Union Hall – the distribution of arms was to extend northwards to the Limerick and Tipperary brigades as well as to Kerry. Routes were selected and the construction of dumps along the routes ordered. Tom Barry and Liam Deasy of Cork No. 3 brigade were selected to implement the decisions. Michael Leahy had gone to Italy in mid-April and was to return on the Italian ship carrying 20,000 rifles, 500 machine guns and 500,000 rounds of ammunition.[3]

The formation into a divisional organisation took place on

26 April 1921 in Lynch's brigade area at Kippagh near Millstreet. Nine brigades were included and at this meeting Liam Lynch was appointed divisional commandant.[4] This responsibility was far greater than that undertaken by any officer outside of Dublin and equalled only by a few officers at GHQ. He then commanded nine brigades comprising more than 30,000 officers and men.[5]

Ernie O'Malley represented GHQ at the meeting and read a memorandum outlining GHQ's conception of divisional functions.[6] According to Tom Barry, the document which he read did not find favour with many of the men: 'Military terminology rolled off his tongue.' The more he continued to speak and use words like 'terrain' and 'topography' the more he angered his listeners.

The men O'Malley was dealing with were shrewd and mentally alert, men like Liam Lynch, Seán Moylan, Humphrey Murphy, Andy Cooney, Tom Barry, Liam Deasy, Dan Breen, John Joe Rice and other well-known names. Seán O'Hegarty commanding Cork No. 1 brigade jumped to his feet and told Ernie O'Malley to shut up. O'Hegarty voiced the bitter feelings, which many of the IRA fighting officers now entertained towards GHQ. He asked why didn't a senior staff officer like Michael Collins or Richard Mulcahy come, indeed, 'why didn't any of these ever think it worth their while to visit any of the active fighting units in the south?' It was a plea of frustration. These men in the Southern Division, in touch with the grass roots of the fight, living daily on their wits now had confirmed what they had for some time believed, that Collins, Mulcahy, and the men at GHQ had no conception of what guerrilla fighting was all about.

As the meeting continued Barry told the meeting that the order from GHQ bore no relation whatever to the realities of the situation in the south. 'There's no point in using ornate language and meaningless military phrases to impress hard-bitten officers who are daily fighting forces against all odds. These men in GHQ don't understand what is required to make split-second decisions when a group of men are in danger of being surrounded. They don't know what quick action is needed when an ambush or barracks' attack doesn't go according to plan." It would not work having brigades moving around in a large battalion when 'the three Cork brigades could hardly muster 300 rifles between them, were without automatic weapons, artillery or transport, had no proper signalling equipment and no proper staff arrangements.'[8]

A close friend of Lynch, Seán Moylan of Cork, shouted, 'We started this war with hurleys, but by heavens it seems to me we will finish it off with fountain pens.'

Nevertheless, the First Southern Division was set up and Lynch now had to accept what the documents stated was 'a grave and solemn responsibility'. In area and numerical strength Lynch's division was more than three times the extent of any division subsequently formed – he now had the IRA in three and a half counties under his command. Hope was expressed at this meeting that the Italian consignment would materialise and transform the entire conflict in the south. Before the meeting closed Barry suggested that something should be done to stop the executions of IRA prisoners. Prisoners were held in the military detention barracks in Cork and a number of executions, after trial by military court, had already taken place. Barry suggested that Major General E. P. Strickland, the British General O/C in the martial law area, should be told that if the IRA's demand was not met that reprisals would be carried out. Four of O'Hegarty's volunteers from Cork and one from the Tipperary area were due for execution before a firing squad in Cork towards the end of April. Liam Lynch undertook to write to General Strickland informing him of their decision. A plan of reprisal was drawn up in case Strickland chose to ignore the warning.

The executions of the four Cork volunteers took place on 28 April 1921 and the plan was immediately put into action. (Simultaneous attacks on all British garrisons in the division on Saturday 14 May at 3 p.m.) Not all the brigades participated in the action. Cork No. 3 under Barry's command was the most successful. Throughout the south it resulted in a higher British casualty list than had ever been the case since Easter Week 1916.

GHQ's lack of consultation with Cork brigades

Liam Lynch realised that a central headquarters would now be necessary for himself and his divisional staff. This was secured at MacSuibhne's house, Coolea – an area where the people were loyal and trustworthy. Not a word of English was spoken in these headquarters and from this isolated spot, lines of communication to all the brigade headquarters and to GHQ were quickly established. This meant the involvement of railway workers, lorry drivers and all who could help in getting dispatches to their destinations. Lynch had put in motion an intricate system to assimilate what had been happening in different areas; for security reasons written orders and directions were kept to a minimum and often coded. Maurice Walshe of Mitchelstown, who had been Lynch's principal staff officer, moved to this area and took up duty.

Lynch's next task was to visit the brigades within a week of his appointment as divisional commander. With Florence O'Donoghue, he travelled at times on foot, at times in pony trap, on horseback or by boat and the entire inspection tour lasted fifteen days. In each of the brigade areas which the two men visited they had meetings with battalion and column commanders:

> Every factor influencing the development of the fight was reviewed in detail – organisation, training, arms, intelligence, supply of explosives, communications, security, availability of men and weapons for columns, leadership and control of all formations down to the companies – all these were examined and orders given for such revisions and changes as were found to be necessary.[1]

Flying columns had come to be accepted as the most effective formation of command while the arms' position remained critical. It was always Lynch's hope that more arms might become available and thus change the situation. For successful guerrilla activity, speed and surprise was translated into success. When evasion was essential to survival, evasion was the correct policy.

It upset Liam to think that the civilian population were often treated savagely, therefore he urged all units to remain vigilant, and impressed on the officers the value of sniping and road-cutting on a well-planned scale. According to Florence O'Donoghue: 'the impact of his vigorous personality and his confident grasp of every fact in a complex situation had a bracing effect. He inspired many officers with a new and wider concept of the task and the objective.'[2]

Upon the formation of the Southern Division Lynch had to undertake responsibility for the administrative and supply problems which a vigorous campaign entailed. While undertaking such a task he continued the policy he operated in his own brigade of giving officers the maximum authority and freedom of action, and of holding them responsible for the results. In order to obtain arms and provision of food and clothing they needed money. He adopted a method of putting a levy based on the Poor Law Valuation of the individual holdings to cover the entire population of each brigade area. This meant that the poor areas bore less of the burden as they were already over-taxed through providing food on a large scale for the men 'on the run'. In the majority of cases the levy was freely given. Similar organisation was undertaken in the nine brigades in his division. However, all suffered from a lack of arms.

In the No. 3 area, the flying column under Tom Barry's command fought a number of successful actions including Crossbarry on 19 March 1921 where 104 officers and men outfought 1,200 British forces by breaking the encirclement and inflicting casualties on the enemy, destroying part of their transport and capturing a large quantity of arms and ammunition.

Lynch, in an effort to maintain a high standard of efficiency in the columns, suggested that all should remember the lessons learned in previous attacks – failures and success alike. He issued some orders and memoranda, an example of which is as follows:

> ... When moving, columns should have advance and rear guards connected with the main body.

> Columns should never move into the country until it is first
> scouted and the O/C has satisfied himself that it is either free of the
> enemy, or is aware of the exact position he occupies.[3]

Lynch undertook all his activities in an efficient manner as can be seen from the many 'Operation Orders' which he issued.[4]

As time progressed, further plans were worked out. On the horizon there was to be the establishment of a divisional training camp at which all brigade officers and column commanders would undergo courses of intensive training. The courses were to be continued for other officers and the whole project visualised the creation of a divisional column for operations. Commandant Tom Barry of Cork No. 3 brigade was to be training officer and was to command the divisional column when formed. The establishment of the camp in Clydagh Valley between Rathmore and Ballyvourney was also being planned. Barry was not in agreement with the idea as he felt that by bringing together so many senior officers, the IRA was running the risk of putting the entire armed effort in the south-west of Ireland in jeopardy. It was his contention that 'if the officers were to be captured or wiped out in a confrontation it would cripple the decision-making of the remaining volunteers as well as being a devastating blow to morale.'[5] He also believed that guerrilla warfare could not be taught. If men, with aggression and initiative, came into the active areas he felt this would be superior to any training camp as they would participate in action. This was the first major disagreement which Barry had with Lynch. However, though Barry disagreed with Liam Lynch's decision on the divisional training camp issue, he was nevertheless prepared to give it a try. With Liam Deasy, Barry was on his way towards the Cork/Kerry border when at the end of the first day's journey a dispatch arrived from Lynch informing them that the area of the proposed camp was infested by the enemy and it would be advisable to wait until the enemy withdrew.

In early May 1921 the extremely fine weather did not favour guerrilla warfare. In certain areas British forces formed a type of mobile unit where ten or twenty men in lorries were dropped in regions under an officer or a senior NCO. They moved across the country silently and quickly with the minimum of equipment to a rendezvous where they were again picked up by their transport. Such activity was a potential threat to individuals and to the IRA communication system. It immobilised many of the volunteers' basic units, destroyed communications and added to their losses as a number of men were killed or captured. The failure of the Italian arms' shipment as well as a large-scale extensive combing of mountainous areas made the task of fighting the crown forces extremely difficult.

In Lynch's area the combined force of Cork No. 2 and Kerry No. 2 brigades ambushed a party of police near the village of Rathmore on 4 May 1921. Eight policemen were killed and their arms and ammunition captured. That night the enemy forces as a reprisal set fire to five farmhouses (four of which were totally destroyed) in the vicinity of the scene of the ambush. Later they burned down Rathmore creamery and Co-operative Stores.

The O'Regan family home, Glenfield, Liscarroll destroyed by crown forces in 1921. Michael O'Regan, his wife Margaret and daughters Julia and Kitty amid the ruins
(Courtesy, Michael McGrath & Peter Somers)

On 1 June a cycle patrol of police was ambushed between Castlemaine and Milltown by Kerry No. 1 brigade under the command of Tadgh Brosnan – six Auxiliaries were killed and five wounded and their ammunition and arms were captured. Under the command of Paddy O'Brien a large-scale action against the crown forces took place on 16 June at Rathcoole (between Millstreet and Banteer) where columns from Millstreet, Kanturk, Newmarket, Charleville and Mallow combined forces. They attacked four lorries of Auxiliaries. One hundred and forty IRA were involved and suffered no casualties. The following day they recovered 1,350 rounds of ammunition which the Auxiliaries had abandoned. This was a great coup for Lynch's brigade.

On the night of 11 May, Paddy O'Brien, his brother Dan and Jack O'Regan were in John O'Donnell's, near Liscarroll, when they were surprised by British troops. The two O'Briens and O'Regan ran out the back way but were fired on. O'Regan was hit and fell. Dan O'Brien and Jack O'Regan were captured. Paddy O'Brien escaped. Dan O'Brien was taken to Cork military barracks, tried by drumhead court-martial and sentenced to death. He was executed on 16 May 1921. That night, when returning from Limerick, Liam Lynch and Florrie O'Donoghue had a narrow escape. They intended reaching Kiskeam, near Mallow, but because their horse was tired they rested for the night near Tuar. In a round-up at Kiskeam, Seán Moylan was captured, and subsequently sentenced to fifteen years penal servitude. Only

Dan O'Brien
(Courtesy, Michael McGrath & Peter Somers)

for the tired horse Liam and Florrie would have slept in the same house with Moylan that night.

Lynch arrived back at division headquarters on 17 May and remained there until 31 May, when he set out to visit the Waterford brigade. Back in headquarters on 14 June he did some book-

work, then left three days later for further visits to brigades. During this period one of the most extensive combing operations undertaken by the British forces had been carried out in the mountainous area enclosed by the circle – Kilgarven, Rathmore, Millstreet, Ballyvourney and Dunmanway. Several thousand lorry-
camping troops supported by armed vehicles and aircraft participated in the operation, which began on 6 June. General Strickland defined their mission as that of 'seeking out the IRA columns,
bringing them to action and annihilating'.

According to the *Morning Post*, 'Information has been received from Ireland that the IRA is being mobilised ... Present
happenings seem clearly to indicate that the rebel army means to
come into the open ... In the wild country around the Clydagh
Mountains, County Kerry, the concentration of a rebel force is in
progress and at least 1,000 are already massed.'[6] It seemed as if
the forces of the crown and the British newspapers were under
the impression that the IRA would come out and attack openly
as they had done in 1916. A week after the appearance of this
news item in the *Morning Post* the sweep began.

Strickland's order was in Lynch's hands almost as soon as it
reached Strickland's own brigade commanders. Though the
weather favoured the British action, broken bridges and trenched
roads hindered their movement, and because of their slow rate
the columns outstripped them. The columns generally moved
under darkness whereas the British forces halted at night. The
Cork columns and Kerry No. 2 column were the main targets.
Good intelligence and prompt reports made it possible to keep
all units informed of the progress of the raiding forces. Divisional
headquarters were centrally situated and were able to send dispatches readily. Though it might have been possible for some of
the columns such as Barry's flying column to break the encirclement, evasion was considered to be a better policy because of the
enormous superiority of the enemy in both men and weapons.

The entire operation did not lead to the capture of even one
IRA member or any weapons or documents though unarmed

civilians in many areas were shot during the action. Some weeks later on 23/24 June, a second large-scale sweep by the British forces enclosed an area, which centred around Millstreet, and it looked as if the authorities had information as to the where-abouts of Lynch's headquarters. Lynch and Joe O'Connor had returned from a tour of Kerry and the West Limerick brigades and arrived at Rathcoole at 4 a.m. Being exhausted they decided to sleep, even though they had been told that they were within 'the British ring'. Paddy O'Brien, also in need of sleep decided to remain on duty. He woke Liam and Joe O'Connor after a few hours as reports indicated that the raiding parties were moving in on all sides in full strength. The IRA men moved into Kilcorney, where they remained for the day, and later in the evening, they moved again. Due to an accurate report, they were able to get out-side the encirclement despite having been within a hair's breath of being captured.

IRA activity was still hampered by fine weather and June saw very little action. By this time rumours of efforts being made to bring about an ending of the conflict were widespread. Despite these rumours Lynch was unable to foresee an end to hostilities. In fact, it appeared as if the British government forces were step-ping up their activity. Though the shortage of arms for the volun-teers was now a biting reality, morale was nevertheless excellent as Lynch discovered in his review of the nine brigades in his division. He anticipated, therefore, that, with the possibility of securing further arms, a resumption of the struggle on a larger scale would be feasible in the autumn.

However, though the possibilities of a truce were being con-sidered by De Valera, Collins, Cathal Brugha and others, Liam Lynch was not consulted as to the capacity of his command to con-tinue the struggle. The only contact headquarters made with any member of the Southern Division was between Michael Collins, De Valera and Tom Barry of Cork No. 3 brigade. Dev asked Barry how long he felt his flying column could maintain the struggle in the field against the British. 'It depends on the British reinforcement and the amount of arms we are able to obtain,' said Dáil̄y, adding that they could last another five years. Dev replied, 'A bit too optimistic'.[7] It was some weeks before Barry was able to meet Lynch and give him information on the conversations which took place at GHQ.

One of the unanswered questions of the period is why Liam Lynch the commanding officer of the First Southern Division was not consulted by GHQ or given an opportunity of expressing his views. More than anybody else he was in a position to assess the situation particularly at this time of mid-June 1921 as he had travelled around to each of the nine brigades in his area over the past number of months on at least two occasions. The First Southern Division was the largest and most active and had played the greatest part in the war; in addition this region had by far the largest concentration of British forces, and the inhabitants had suffered a great deal because of their involvement.

Piaras Beaslaí, in his book *Michael Collins and the Making of a New Ireland*, stated that Liam Lynch and some of his officers went to GHQ some time before the truce and reported that owing to shortage of arms, ammunition and enemy pressure they were unable to continue the fight.[8] This statement was inaccurate. Florence O'Donoghue of No. 2 brigade confirmed that he had seen a letter from Liam Lynch in which he asked for 'a few rifles' and said, 'We will soon be in a very bad way for .303 as we had hard luck in captures recently.' Another letter from Cork No. 3 read that they were urgently in need of .303, adding 'to a certain extent we are held up by the want of this and harassed to a terrible extent by the enemy.' O'Donoghue was aware that Liam Lynch had not been directly consulted for an opinion, and believed it was untrue that they were 'unable to continue the fight' as Beaslaí had stated. (O'Donoghue accepted Beaslaí's assurance that his original statement was made in good faith and under a misapprehension of the facts.)[9]

Tom Barry, in *Guerrilla Days in Ireland*, said, 'No deputation of southern officers ever visited GHQ ... It is a fact that Lynch never left the First Southern Division area in all those months. Furthermore, no brigade or battalion officer from Kerry, Cork or Waterford brigades visited Dublin or GHQ between the end of March and the truce except myself towards the end of May and Seán Buckley in May ... Every Divisional and Brigade officer in the south rejects completely Beaslaí's statement about Liam Lynch.'[10]

Shortage of arms was, of course, an acute problem. Complications had arisen with the shipment of arms which was being organised by Donal Hales in Italy. Madge Hales, Donal's sister, went to Italy and personally returned to Collins with information of the cancellation of the shipment.[11] As Madge Hales' dispatch was by word of mouth, and, because of the usual secrecy in IRA circles, she did not inform anybody else, but it does seem extraordinary that Michael Collins did not pass the information on to either Tom Barry or to Liam Deasy who were organising the intake, transport and dumps, together with the scouts along the route, and also that he did not inform Liam Lynch who was the commander of the First Southern Division and to whom the receipt of the proposed shipment of arms was of vital importance.

There is no doubt that Collins was aware of the important role played by the flying columns in the Cork brigades and other southern regions. Nevertheless, these men in the south had not been consulted about their true positions and their true intentions for the future. Were there some seeds sown here which were to spring to life at a later stage during the Civil War when men like Deasy, Barry, Lynch and other officers decided to continue the conflict?

It does appear as if Lynch, Barry, Deasy and other officers in the Southern Division, while they would have welcomed a truce, would only have welcomed a short truce. They were prepared to continue the fight, which they felt would bring success, as their intelligence service was now superior to that of the British. They had people inside the corridors of power transmitting information to the IRA. Years later, Barry, Deasy and many men who were involved in the fight for independence, were convinced that had there been a shorter truce followed by a renewal of the armed conflict, the British might have been forced to enter into a more meaningful treaty which, with hindsight, could possibly have stopped the Civil War. The IRA was, by this time, tougher, more experienced and more immune to hardship. Extra men were coming on full-time active service: combat experience was more widespread, and with the majority of the civilian population behind them the columns were able to move more freely. Food and clothing for the men on active duty was provided by Cumann na mBan and houses throughout all brigade areas became safe billeting depots.

Truce – hope for full settlement

In 1920 and the first half of 1921 the British establishment gave the Black and Tans and Auxiliaries free reign in Ireland when they allowed them to terrorise the Irish people. They browbeat, insulted, murdered and maimed civilians as well as the IRA in order to create a climate of despair.

In *Ireland For Ever* Brigadier General Crozier said, 'Never before had the RIC been used so ruthlessly and at times surreptitiously, to destroy and create a new note of anguish in the country.'[1] Not alone did terror fail but public opinion in England disliked what was happening.

Early in April 1921 Lord French gave an interview to the *Daily Express* in which he admitted that the volunteers were an army 'properly organised in regiment and brigade, led by disciplined officers.' Significant also was the fact that their voluntary army had taken the initiative and was confronting the occupation forces with many new, unexpected tactics. The British government discovered that the tactics adopted kept their forces under a perpetual strain. This type of guerrilla warfare was totally at variance with anything that they had previously experienced.

British foreign relations in America and elsewhere were beginning to incur disfavour, therefore their alternative was to use unlimited military force under a reign of martial law or to engage in some form of settlement. General Macready suggested to the British government that, if a solution was not reached by July, martial law would be imposed throughout the entire country with the exception of the Ulster counties. This would mean reinforcing the garrison with an additional nineteen battalions and a strong force of marines. British army strength in Ireland would then be brought to 80,000 men, but he felt 150,000 would be essential if a military regime were to succeed.[2] Field Marshal Sir Henry Wilson, the chief of the imperial general staff from 1918 to 1921 wrote:

18 May 1921. I said that directly England was safe, every available man should go to Ireland that even four battalions now serving on the Rhine ought also to go to Ireland. I said that the measures taken up to now had been quite inadequate, that I was terrified at the state of the country, and that in my opinion, unless we crushed out the murder gang this summer we shall lose Ireland and the Empire.[3]

Winston Churchill, then secretary of state for the colonies, told the cabinet:

One hundred thousand new special troops must be raised, thousands of motorcars must be armed and equipped; the three southern provinces of Ireland must be closely laced with cordons of blockades and barbed wire: a systematic rummaging and questioning of every individual must be put in force.

But towards the end of June it was obvious to the British that some form of compromise was necessary. The lord chancellor, Lord Birkenhead, speaking in the British House of Lords on 24 June 1921 said:

... if I must speak frankly, I think that the history of the last three months has been the history of the failure of our military method to keep pace with and overcome the military methods which have been taken by our opponents.

C. J. C. Street, imperial activist, intelligence officer and advisor to Lloyd George wrote later:

There were only two alternatives, to come to terms with Sinn Féin or exterminate its armed forces.[4]

The British forces did not seem to be able to exterminate or to beat the Irish volunteers and a truce was declared.

Liam Lynch was at division HQ at Coolea when official notification of a truce reached him on 10 July 1921. Immediately he issued the necessary order for the cessation of hostilities in his brigade to come into force at 12 noon the next day.

Were it not for this order his former brigade might have pulled off the greatest success in his region. Paddy O'Brien with eighty officers and men from five battalion columns had some days previously marched into West Limerick and, in co-operation with West Limerick units, laid an ambush near Templeglantine. For several days the column had lain in wait without finding a target. But they were prepared to wait.

Upon receipt of notification O'Brien called his section commanders together and asked for their views regarding taking up positions on the morning of 11 July 1921. All were eager to do so, and the column went into position. At 11.35 the column commander instructed the section commanders to withdraw their sections. The truce was to come into being at 12 o'clock. At 12.15 the British convoy arrived on the scene and passed some of the dispersing groups on the road; not a shot was fired. The struggle towards agreement was now in the hands of the diplomats.

During the previous years, many volunteers throughout Ireland had displayed courage and determination, had fought and died for the Republic. But the south had earned a Republic more than any other part of Ireland. In Liam Lynch's division, 193 officers and men were killed, twice that number wounded and about 2,000 interned or sentenced to terms of imprisonment. In the face of those losses they had, under many other and varied difficulties, continued to strike at the occupation forces so vigorously and persistently that responsible British military commanders were convinced of the necessity for immense reinforcements if their defeat was to be achieved.

In the March 1921, issue of *An tÓglach* a tribute was paid to the men of the south. 'The Cork brigades have proved themselves to have reached a level of military efficiency which make them a match for the most highly trained soldiers in the world. An example has been set which every brigade in Ireland should strive to emulate.'[5]

The first reaction to the truce was one of optimism. Officers and men in Lynch's division had for the previous eighteen months concentrated their attention and energy upon the fight to such an extent that all other considerations, personal and national, were excluded. In their optimism, the people of the south believed that England had at last decided, in calling a truce, to evacuate her armed forces from the country, and that this would lead to the establishment of a freely functioning Republic.

Men close to Liam Lynch later expressed their opinion that in Lynch's view the truce came a little too soon; however Lynch expected that the respite would be short and that soon the conflict would be renewed. It was his belief that England was not yet ready for a full settlement and as he continually said he would not contemplate the possibility of any settlement on terms which gave Ireland less than sovereign independence. 'We are and must be prepared to fight to the last for that,' he wrote in a letter to his brother, Tom. 'In justice to the yet unborn as well as to the dead past we have no other authority but to fight on a fight thank God which never for generations seemed more hopeful than now as the Empire is heaving with trouble ...'[6]

Collins' offer – commander-in-chief position

An air of relaxation and a general feeling of freedom and optimism permeated the countryside during the summer of 1921. With the termination of curfew and of the prohibition of fairs and markets, movement and a form of order was restored. Normal trade and commerce created a sense of relief in the public mind. Men who had been out on active service over the past years were at last free to go about without being hampered in their activities. But as time progressed and negotiations in London between the Irish and British delegates proceeded, a dispassionate assessment of the situation was to become more difficult. As far as Liam Lynch was concerned the fight against the British government was not yet over. Quick to realise the danger of apathy, he started to combat any tendency towards relaxation in his division. Training camps were established and an expanded series of inspections were inaugurated. He discouraged men, as far as it was possible, from coming out into the open.

British tact showed itself in the establishment of liaison officers. These were appointed by both sides to supervise the observance of the terms of the truce. By doing so they recognised the IRA as an army and not as a group of rebellious civilians. During this truce period division HQ had been moved from its wartime location at Sweeneys, Coolea to O'Sullivans, Lombardstown on 2 July.

Liam had had very little contact with home over the past year and he now returned home for his brother's ordination on 11 June and stayed for two days. He was again able to meet his girlfriend, Bridie Keyes and the pair had much to discuss, including the prospect of marriage. His hope was that future discussions between both governments would reach a final settlement, and that his days of guerilla warfare would be finally over, so that he could at last settle down and have a future with Bridie. He was thankful to have survived the War of Independence, but sensed an anti-climax.

Richard Mulcahy, chief-of-staff, visited him at division HQ in early August and during the following week the two men inspected units of the Cork and Kerry brigades. Later that month De Valera visited division HQ and, with Liam and a few more officers, over the following three days, made a tour of the scene of the principal actions in the division. At each place the columns, which had participated were mobilised under arms and congratulated by De Valera. Liam was proud and happy. There was no sign of a break in national unity. The future seemed hopeful. Even the *Irish Times* acknowledged a changed Ireland!

> For good or evil the old Ireland is gone. Instead of this there is a young people with new qualities and also with new defects ... none of the efforts that have been made to divide the people have succeeded. On the contrary, they have vindicated the strength of the national ideal.

On the evening of 18 August 1921, Liam was driving back from Bandon when he was held up at Ballinhassig by three cars of military personnel. The district inspector in charge demanded that he produce a British permit for use of the car (one of the restrictions enforced under martial law). Liam demanded the right, as an Irish army officer, to use his own transport without an enemy permit just as British officers 'do without our permits'. Nevertheless, he was taken to Bandon barracks and detained there until 1.30 next day, when, following a phone message from Dublin Castle, he and his driver were released.

Afterwards, he wrote to his brother, 'I enjoyed the time with the Tans and the D.I. as the truce feeling prevailed all round. We even discussed the possibility of again meeting them face to face in a clash with arms.'[1]

But Liam still felt that the truce was only temporary. Planning to go to a dance in Mitchelstown, to meet old friends, especially Bridie Keyes, he wrote, 'I believe that after a few weeks I may have a poor chance of seeing them again. It is also my intention to run home if possible.'[2] His brother Tom came home shortly after the truce and Liam, excusing himself for not being home on that occasion, wrote, 'somehow I would consider it a national sin when there is work to be done.'

With Seán Moylan, Liam was on his way to Dublin for Tom Barry's wedding when his car broke down. They arrived late, so they weren't present for the historic photograph on 22 August 1921. But it was a memorable, social occasion.

After a visit to Dublin in mid-September, he expressed a feeling to his comrades that national unity was within sight 'though there may be a resumption of the struggle in arms.'[3]

To his brother Tom he wrote:

> You may rest assured that our government as well as the army is out for the Republic and nothing less, and that without a rest on our oars either. We are and must be prepared to fight to the last for that ...[4]

Subsequent to the assembly of the second Dáil in the Mansion House, Dublin, De Valera and Lloyd George entered into a series of communications. On 14 September Dáil Éireann sanctioned the appointment of delegates and negotiations commenced in London on 11 October 1921. (The Irish delegates were Arthur Griffith, Michael Collins, George Gavan-Duffy, Robert Barton and Éamon Duggan.)[5]

It was October before Liam was again able to visit home. On this occasion he went to Ballylanders Races. Congratulations were heaped on him by locals, but Liam viewed the newfound patriotism of many with a jaundiced eye:

> I don't give a damn about these people when it comes to praise or notoriety, and they are making the hell of a mistake if they think I forget their actions during the war. I remember at one time in the best areas where it was next to impossible to find a bed to lie on.'[6]

Liam appeared happiest when he was among army men as within the movement he found warmth and friendship. He balanced the integrity of the men within the conflict with the insincerity of some of those who were outside.

He spent much of October and November in IRA organisational activities and conferences both in the Southern Division and at GHQ. His ability and integrity impressed the Dáil cabinet so much, that at the end of November 1921, he was offered the position as commander-in-chief of the army. (This would mean Richard Mulcahy, chief-of-staff, would be sub-ordinate to him.)

As Michael Collins and his comrades wrestled in London with the culmination of the treaty debates, Liam apparently anticipating the resumption of war against Britain, wrote to Cathal Brugha:

> Headquarters,
> 1st Southern Division,
> 6th December, 1921.
>
> To the Minister for Defence
> It is after serious consideration I acquaint you that I cannot under present circumstances accept the commission you offer me.
> I feel that the Commander-in-Chief and his staff cannot do their duty when they are not placed in a position to do so. I may have wrong views of the duties of a Commander-in-Chief and Minister for Defence, if so I will put up with the result. I painfully realise the consequences of the present relations between Cabinet and GHQ Staff, therefore I cannot act blindly in the matter and be responsible for directing general operation policy. At the present moment when war may be resumed at short notice I have got no general directions.
> When the situation is cleared up to the Brigade Commandants in this Division I shall be pleased to be relieved of my present responsibility.
>
> Liam Lynch Commandant.[7]

This letter from Lynch seems to imply that tension existed between the cabinet and GHQ, and that Lynch at this period and subsequently maintained that control of the army should be free from cabinet interference.

On 6 December 1921 the Articles of Agreement for a treaty – which required an oath of allegiance to a British monarch disestablished the Republic and partitioned Ireland – were signed. Where British arms had failed, British diplomacy had won. A chapter in Irish history was closed and another, more bitter was about to begin.

IRB's allegiance to the Republic

Liam Lynch became a member of the Irish Republican Brotherhood late in 1918 when he formed a circle in Fermoy. The following year he gathered up some threads of the organisation and was elected as its centre.

The Irish Republican Brotherhood (IRB) was a secret oathbound society founded in 1858 when John O'Mahony and Michael Doheny, acting on behalf of a group of exiled young Irelanders in the United States sent Owen Considine to James Stephens in Ireland with proposals for the foundation of the organisation, and promises of support from America.[1]

John O'Mahony had been born near Liam's homeplace, and Liam had studied his activities from an early age. The seven signatories of the proclamation of the Republic at Easter 1916 were the members of the IRB military council. (The constitution provided for the establishment of a military council subordinate to the supreme council.) The executions after Easter Week 1916 almost wiped out the supreme council. However in the autumn of 1917 the council was regularly constituted with Seán McGarry as president, Michael Collins as secretary and Diarmuid Lynch as treasurer. Even after the reconstitution of the supreme council no active steps were implemented to revitalise the organisation, mainly because De Valera and Brugha had come to the conclusion that there was no longer a necessity for the continuance of a secret organisation as they felt the future of the national struggle for independence could now be staked upon open military and political organisations. Michael Collins, however, believed the continued existence of the secret organisation was essential in achieving a Republic. In this he was supported by members like Liam Lynch.

The south Munster division of the IRB consisted of the counties of Cork, Kerry and Waterford. The supreme council requested Lynch to act as divisional officer in March 1921 to re-place Tom Hales who had been arrested.[2] Lynch agreed, thus he automatically gained a seat on the supreme council – a body which regarded itself as the guardian of Republican policy. This event took place shortly before the enlarged formation of the First Southern Division of the IRA of which he was given leadership. Between March and December 1921 the South Munster Division of the IRB, under his direction, had been re-organised, and its membership increased.

When the Articles of Agreement for the treaty were signed in London the organisation was galvanised into activity. The IRB would have to take a stand. The supreme council met following the signing, and issued a note to all divisions around the country:

> The Organisation
> The Peace Treaty
> The Supreme Council having due regard to the Constitution of the Organisation, has decided that the present Peace Treaty between Ireland and Great Britain should be ratified. Members of the Organisation, however, who have to take public action as re-presentatives are given freedom of action in the matter.[3]

This meeting, held on the night of 10 December 1921, was Liam's first as a member of the supreme council. Two letters record his reaction. The next day he wrote to Florence O'Donoghue:

> The situation is that I stood alone at the meeting I attended, and our Division seemingly stands alone in the army. GHQ staff and several others who have done actual army work are for the Treaty ... My belief is that the Treaty will be carried by a majority of the Dáil. The position I have taken up I mean to stand by, even if the whole division turn it down. On the other hand I do not recom-mend immediate war as our front is broken – which our leaders are responsible for ...[4]

Referring to Michael Collins, he wrote, 'I admire Mick as a sol-dier and a man. Thank God all parties can agree to differ.'[5]

This letter to Florence O'Donoghue and the following letter he wrote to his brother Fr Tom express his foremost ideal that his initial goal was an Irish Republic. The content of these letters should be borne in mind as one views the turn which events began to take over the year ahead. Because of his generosity of spirit he appears to have over-estimated this quality in others:

> First of all I must assure you that my attitude is now as always, to fight on for the recognition of the Republic. Even if I were to stand alone I will not voluntarily accept being part of the British Empire.
>
> Whatever will happen here in this week of destiny we must and will show a united front. Thank God that we can agree to differ. Minority of the Dáil will stand by majority no matter what side, the same will apply to the army. Therefore there will be no disunity as in the past.
>
> It is only natural that in such a big issue there would be a difference of opinion ... All my Division hold the one view, and that strongly too. Several other southern areas, I know already, are with us in this view. If the government accept the Treaty we shall not, but strike for final victory at most favourable opportunity.
>
> There is no allegiance asked to the British Empire, only to be faithful to it. At all times of course, we give allegiance to the Irish Constitution ... The Governor-General would be of our own choice say for instance Count Plunkett, and he certainly, as only a figurehead would not be much of a connection for king ...
>
> Even if we must temporarily accept the Treaty there is scarcely another leap to freedom ...
>
> Speeches and fine talk do not go far these days. We have already too much gas, what we want is a definite line of action ...
>
> Sorry I must agree to differ with Collins – that does not make us worse friends ...[6]

Dáil deputies who were members of the supreme council were free to vote for or against the treaty, but those who were against ratification were put in the position of acting in opposition to the wishes of the council.

The South Munster Division received the decision taken by the Dáil with amazement as well as anger. At the autumn elections before the opening of the London negotiations, Michael Collins had come to Cork and presided at the divisional meeting when Liam Lynch was elected divisional centre officer. The men who met in O'Briens, Parnell Place, were representative of the mind and spirit of both organisations in the area. Michael Collins spoke to Liam and some other officers just before the meeting and he gave, in general terms, the first indication that some modification of the full Republican demand might have to be made in the London negotiations if a settlement was to be reached. Lynch asked Collins not to repeat this at the meeting or else it would 'blow up'.[7] He did, however, state that the officers had fully earned the right to be consulted before any final decision was reached on whatever terms of settlement were proposed by the British, and, as far as he was concerned, he would do his best to see that it was carried out.[8] Everybody was satisfied. However no further communication reached them until the supreme council's decision (Michael Collins was chairman) was issued to division and country centres on 12 December after the treaty had been signed.

The day the council's decision was made Cork district board met and called for 'the rejection of the Treaty proposal being submitted to Dáil Éireann as being utterly at variance with the principles of the IRB and treason to the Republic established in 1916.'[9]

Liam, in a letter to his brother, explained, 'my attitude is now as always to fight on for the recognition of the Republic ... At all times we give allegiance to the Irish constitution ... we can scarcely realise what a fine country Ireland will be when freedom comes ...'[10]

On 7 January 1922 the Cork county centre IRB reported to Lynch that the entire membership of the organisation in the city and county was unanimously opposed to acceptance of the treaty proposals. Similar reports from the county organisations of Kerry and Waterford arrived soon afterwards. On 12 January the supreme council issued a statement to its IRB members which suggested that no action for or against the present peace treaty be taken by the organisation as such, so that the final attainment of 'A Free Independent Republican Government in Ireland' could be achieved; but the council also issued a statement to Dáil Éireann members wherein it suggested that 'the present Peace Treaty between Ireland and Great Britain should be ratified. Members of the organisation, however, who have to take public action as representatives are given freedom of action in the matter ...'

The document, which appeared to give other members freedom of choice, split the organisation. All the south Munster division rejected it. Lynch saw a conflict and a rejection of all he had fought for; he believed that, in making this decision, the supreme council ignored the fact that the whole national position had been changed. With a passionate intensity he resented the fact that any group of new, though chosen, leaders would attempt to destroy what they had sworn to uphold in the declaration of the Republic in 1916, and also by the solemn ratification of it by the people at two subsequent general elections. 'The people have been stampeded, owing to war-weariness and threat of extermination by the enemy. In cooler moments, they will keenly realise that indescribable spirit of nationality and again stand up with their heads high,' he wrote to his brother.[11] A crisis was imminent. Not alone was there conflict within the supreme council of the IRB, there was also conflict within the cabinet.

President de Valera and Cathal Brugha, minister for defence, wished to strengthen the constitutional position by a more explicit expression of the absolute subordination of the army to the government, a situation which existed nominally since March. Liam Lynch however regarded absolute cabinet control of the army with considerable misgivings. He feared that whatever military strength existed in the nation would be reduced to near impotence by British government control.

Dáil Éireann which debated the treaty had resumed its sitting after the Christmas recess on 3 January 1922. Liam Deasy records that Florrie O'Donoghue, Liam Lynch and himself had been invited to sit in on public debates which were held in Dublin '... day after sad day we had our first political experience which was unforgettable and most distressing. We had to listen to men who a few short months before were fighting as comrades side by side now indulging in bitter recrimination, rancour, invective, charges and counter-charges. Gone was the old chivalry

... This meant that many of our dreams and hopes for Ireland's freedom were being shattered."[12]

First indication of treaty split

The vote on the treaty was taken on 7 January 1922. Sixty-four Dáil deputies voted for acceptance, fifty-seven against. Two days later President de Valera resigned. Arthur Griffith was elected in his place. National unity was broken. On 14 January, the sixty-four pro-treaty members met in the Mansion House, approved the treaty and under the chairmanship of Michael Collins elected a Provisional Government which, under the provisions of the British act, was to hold office until 6 December 1922. The British authorities formally handed over control to this Provisional Government on the same day. The British immediately began to withdraw their forces; throughout the country as barracks were vacated they were taken over by the local IRA formations.

Mallow, the second military barracks manned by the Seventeenth Lancers, was handed over by the British on 17 February 1922; for Liam Lynch this was a historic occasion. (The barracks had been captured at mid-day on 28 September 1920 by the Second Cork column led by Lynch and had yielded much-needed ammunition.) Exhilarated, he led a company of armed volunteers through the streets of Mallow amidst cheering crowds; as he passed in through the barrack entrance the British guard presented arms. Many of the original raiding party were with him that day including Dick Willis and Jack Bolster, who had been working inside the barracks as painters in September 1920. Paddy McCarthy who, in 1920, posed as a contractor's overseer had since been killed in action.[1] It was indeed a proud day for Liam Lynch who walked in as an army officer performing a mere routine act of military duty.

Following the Dáil vote on the treaty the senior army officers opposed to its acceptance held a series of consultations. Lynch was among this group who wished to adopt a policy where the army would revert to its original status as a volunteer force under the control of an elected Executive. In order to put this into operation a convention for the election of this Executive had to be held without delay. With the exception of Frank Aiken, O/C Fourth Northern Division, it was finally agreed that an army convention would be held within two months from that date. (18 January 1922) Richard Mulcahy, now minister for defence, gave a personal undertaking that the army would be maintained as the army of the Irish Republic. Lynch attended a conference of GHQ and divisional commandants and commanding officers of brigades which was held in Dublin on 24 February, at which the convention was fixed for 26 March. Preparation of an agenda for the convention was deferred to a meeting of the same officers to be held on 15 March. Meanwhile in anticipation of army unity being maintained officers and men were to go to Beggars Bush barracks for specialised training.

The minister for defence was to ask for permission to hold an army convention when the Dáil re-assembled on 28 February 1922. However, it was decided by the cabinet to sanction the minister's request and not to bring it before the Dáil. This gave all the indications of army unity, despite the growing expansion of a distinct pro-treaty force with headquarters at Beggars Bush barracks, which now housed a number of officers and men from all parts of the country.

Lynch was happy that agreement had been reached at the Sinn Féin Ard Fheis on 21 February between De Valera and Austin Stack on the one side and Arthur Griffith and Michael Collins (Provisional Government) on the other. This implied unity of the political wing; it was agreed that Dáil Éireann would continue to function as it did before the signing of the treaty, its existing president and cabinet remaining in office. Further to this no election would be held during that period and when the electorate voted on the treaty, they would also vote on the constitution. This agreement was ratified on 2 March by Dáil Éireann. Happy at what appeared to be a development towards unity, Lynch returned to his divisional headquarters at Mallow. Conscious of the preservation of army unity he was determined that the force would continue its allegiance to the Republic and remain unchanged in its voluntary capacity. Lynch wanted the army of the Republic to function not alone in the posts being evacuated by the British but also in those which they still continued to occupy in the northern counties.

On 18 February Liam Forde, mid-Limerick brigade, issued a proclamation repudiating the authority of GHQ. Because he took over the evacuating barracks, GHQ ordered Michael Brennan, of the First Western Division who favoured the treaty, to move detachments from Clare into the city to take over posts being evacuated. It was an unusual move and the first time that one brigade was ordered into another area. A dangerous situation was about to develop. Captain Hurley who was brigade quartermaster of mid-Limerick decided to organise a separate force and take back from the First Western Division the area they had taken. He brought in anti-treaty men from Tipperary, Cork and elsewhere, and on 5 March a parade was held. Hurley was placed under arrest. Between 6 and 10 March a number of anti-treaty units moved into Limerick, occupied hotels and a wing of the mental hospital. Pro-treaty groups were also, at the time, occupying some of the evacuated British posts in the city whilst British forces were quartered in others. The situation was explosive. The threat of Civil War hung over Limerick. Many people, including the mayor of Limerick, tried to reconcile the conflicting elements and, because they were unsuccessful, Liam Lynch and Oscar Traynor were called to a meeting with Mulcahy, Michael Collins and O'Duffy at Beggars Bush, which resulted in Liam Lynch being asked to intervene. With Oscar Traynor, O/C Dublin brigade, Lynch went to Limerick and worked out a solution to the problem. Because of adverse publicity he felt it necessary to give the correct facts to the press in a letter dated 27 April 1922:

> I have always avoided publicity but my name has been brought forward so much recently that I am reluctantly forced to deal with the matter.

Regarding the statement by Beggars Bush headquarters to the effect that they had done everything for unity in the army and that the other side had done everything possible to break it, I am sure all officers and high command in the Free State forces can verify my emphatic assertion that no officers did more than myself to maintain a united army.

My activity with O/C Dublin brigade in forcing the Limerick settlement when all others, including the Mayor of Limerick, had failed, is sufficient proof of this, and I am sure that Limerick's first citizen will bear out what I say. The M.D. and Mr Collins were present when agreement was reached. In accordance with the terms of agreement in that most serious situation Owen O'Duffy C/S authorised me in writing:

To hand over to the charge of the Limerick corporation the four police barracks, and

To install a small maintenance party – responsible to myself – in the two military barracks, releasing the occupying troops to return to their areas.

Revolvers taken would be returned.

Mr Griffith tried hard to press the issue in a manner which would have resulted in fearful slaughter in the streets of Limerick. I was more pleased with my success in securing an amicable settlement of the Limerick situation than with any victory in connection with my activities in the war.

It was a happy consummation for me to see about 700 armed troops on each side who were about to engage in mortal combat, eventually leave Limerick as comrades. It was the junior officers of the old GHQ staff, who mutinied against the arrangements agreed to by their senior officers in doing the right thing in Limerick, really brought about the present condition of affairs, for I state definitely that it was their action on that occasion which ultimately resulted in a cancellation of the Convention.[2]

Lynch endeavoured to seek a solution to the problem of army allegiance so that Civil War could be averted. He looked to a future convention with hope, but believed if it was to succeed in its main objects with what he saw as a pro-treaty point of view, the army should, in future, be independent of any government. But, being realistic, he was aware of the difficulty a democratic government would have in accepting that it was not in control of the only military force within the country. He felt this situation had arisen because the Dáil had accepted the treaty by a majority vote and in doing so had abandoned its allegiance to the Republic. However, he thought that this was no more than a temporary measure as eventually the treaty would be put to the people for acceptance or rejection.

During all this period his relations with Michael Collins and Richard Mulcahy continued to be friendly. So obvious was his concern for the nation's welfare and the future of the army that no one, however much in disagreement with his views, could treat him with anything other that respect. Being in command of a division (First Southern) which represented in numerical strength more than one-fourth of the entire army, his position was strong. The men under his control had by this time a substantial number of weapons, they had fighting experience and leadership which was even greater than that of many other regions. In addition, the men under his command were unanimous in their opposition to the treaty and they were well aware that he would use his position only in the best interests of the entire nation.

Army conventions – Executive chief-of-staff appointment

In early March 1922, Liam Lynch sought some method of reconciliation between those who were pro-treaty and anti-treaty. He travelled to Dublin accompanied by Florence O'Donoghue, for one of the many meetings which he had with Richard Mulcahy, defence minister and chief-of-staff, O'Duffy, and other GHQ members. The first meeting extended over several days during which the position of the army was reviewed in detail and an effort of compromise was sought so that both opposing points of view could be reconciled. Though public statements from a number of people began to appear in the press showing a partisan view, nevertheless, these men spoke in an atmosphere of goodwill. All of them wished to maintain and foster the atmosphere of co-operation which had prevailed during the long struggle for freedom. Then events suddenly changed. While a meeting of officers was in session preparing the convention agenda, the decision of a cabinet order was conveyed to them:

> It is quite evident to the unanimous Dáil Cabinet that at an Army Convention contemplated for 26 March it is proposed to endeavour to remove the army from under the control of the Government elected by the Irish people, which is Dáil Éireann. Such a purpose is illegal, and you are hereby instructed that the holding of this Convention is illegal.[1]

This immediately terminated efforts to find common ground for the resolutions to be submitted to the convention; Lynch was saddened as he could find no valid reason for the prohibition. The decision of two weeks earlier had been reversed when on 15 March 1922 the cabinet, believing that the majority of the army were opposed to the acceptance of the treaty, initiated the chain of events which precipitated the split.

It would be difficult to speculate what would have happened had the cabinet allowed the convention to be held as had first been agreed. The entire army would have been represented regardless of the viewpoint which each individual held. They would have met in an atmosphere of freedom in keeping with its spirit and tradition. During the previous years it had been cemented into such an organised body and a disciplined force that it should have been possible to arrive at a compromise. As it happened, forbidding the holding of the convention was looked upon by a large number of officers and men as being unjust and unreasonable. (It should be noted that the Provisional Government did not, at this time, make any order. The order was made by the Dáil cabinet.)

Lynch and other anti-treaty officers again met. They decided to hold the convention on the date originally fixed. Irrespective of what views delegates held, they summoned all the already elected delegates of the army to attend the convention. In the document which they issued to the delegates they stated that:

> ... On 18 January last a general Convention of the IRA was sanctioned by the Minister for Defence of the Dáil cabinet, to be held not later than the end of March:
> And whereas as that agreement has been broken by the acquiescence of the Minister for Defence in the instructions issued by President Griffith prohibiting the holding of such a Convention;
> Therefore be it resolved that we, the undersigned members of GHQ Staff and commandants and other officers of the IRA units, hereby call the aforesaid Convention, to be held on the date already determined, Sunday 26 March 1922; the representation to be as set forth in the general order already issued by GHQ.

Fifty-two signatures, including that of Liam Lynch, were added to the document. Lynch who had been in Dublin, hurried back to Mallow for a meeting of the First Southern Division council which was held on 20 March. Unexpectedly Mulcahy (minister for defence) and O'Duffy (chief-of-staff) attended which showed the importance they placed on this division but 'when differences became acute, they both left for Dublin before an agreement was reached'. All present were conscious of the disaster towards which the army was being driven. From the long meeting

112

two important points emerged:

(a) All were adamant that despite the Dáil ban the convention of the army would be held: but they would be willing to postpone the date to later than 26 March so that the entire army could be represented.

(b) The recruiting for the civic guards which was being implemented by the Provisional Government should cease. (This particularly angered a large number of army members.)

After this meeting, Lynch and Liam Deasy, the divisional adjutant, travelled on the following night to Dublin by the mail train and put the proposals which emerged from the First Southern Division council before Arthur Griffith and Michael Collins. Both main clauses were turned down.[2] On the same day, Rory O'Connor gave an interview to the press in which he claimed to represent 80% of the army who were against the treaty. He stated:

The holding of the Convention means that we repudiate the Dáil. If a government goes wrong we must take the consequences ... The Dáil, in deciding that the Irish Republic shall go into the British Empire, has committed an act of national dishonour that we won't stand.

Florence O'Donoghue in summing up Lynch's point of view said, 'It is reasonably certain that they [Rory O'Connor's views] did not accurately represent Liam Lynch's position.'[3]

The convention assembled in the Mansion House, Dublin, on Sunday 26 March 1922. Fifty-four delegates from the First Southern Division (a quarter of the total number of 211) attended the convention. In order to maintain a neutral attitude, Frank Aiken, Fourth Northern Division, did not attend. Liam Mellows presided at the meeting during which a resolution was passed unanimously:

That the army reaffirm its allegiance to the Irish Republic.

That it shall be maintained as the army of the Irish Republic under an Executive appointed by the Convention.

That the army shall be under the supreme control of such Executive which shall draft a constitution for submission to a Convention to be held on 9 April.[4]

A sixteen member Executive was elected to hold office until the adjourned convention assembled two weeks later. Liam Lynch headed the poll in the voting for this Executive and five officers from his division were also elected. The Executive appointed Lynch as chief-of-staff and agreed to set up headquarters at Barry's Hotel.

Two days later (28 March) they issued a statement declaring that the minister for defence and his chief-of-staff at Beggar's Bush no longer exercised any control over the army. The Executive called for the cessation of recruiting for the force, which was being organised by the Provisional Government, and also for an end to civil guard recruiting.

The following day the Executive ordered the destruction of the *Freeman's Journal* machinery following what it termed as 'Misleading Reports of the Convention'.[5] Battalion parades of all units were ordered by the Executive to assemble on Sunday 2 April. At this assembly they reaffirmed their allegiance to the Republic, and Lynch read a statement giving the background to the holding of the convention and the decisions made there.

On Sunday 9 April the army convention reassembled at the Mansion House:

(a) to adopt the Constitution from a draft which had been prepared by the temporary Executive elected at the previous
   Convention.
(b) to elect an Executive to control the army.

In the constitution the wording of the original oath of allegiance, which all volunteers had taken in 1920 pledging allegiance to Dáil Éireann, was amended to pledge to 'support and defend the Irish Republic against all enemies foreign and domestic ...'

In the election of a sixteen member Executive to control the army, Liam headed the poll, was appointed chief-of-staff and included on the newly set-up army council of seven members.[6] With his staff in headquarters at Barry's Hotel his main preoccupation was the split, as conditions of near chaos existed in the army and throughout many parts of the country.

In a letter to his brother Tom which he wrote on 18 April, he said that, 'since the Truce it has been ... a worse time on me than the whole war. Every bribe and cunning plan has been put up to us, but thank God we pulled through to take once more free action ... sad it is to risk having to clash with our old comrades, but we cannot count the cost.'[7]

The situation in which Liam Lynch found himself was more difficult than any he had experienced during the previous years of his life. He worked day and night, very often without rest. He had to wrestle with the anguish which his duties as chief-of-staff of the IRA demanded. 'You need not be troubled by my lofty position as I think nothing of it,' he wrote to his brother. 'I have tried to resign several times during the past few months; but same would not be accepted ... At the moment I am fed up of army and people and were it not for *Ireland's Sake Alone* I would drop out of things. I know my service at the moment is sorely needed.'[8]

The Executive and the portion of the army which gave allegiance to this body had now cut itself off from any share of arms or equipment which had been handed over by the British to the Provisional Government. Parts of this army occupied various barracks and posts throughout the country but they had no financial resources. They had a substantial number of arms which were taken in a raid on Clonmel barracks by anti-treaty forces, otherwise, throughout the country, they were dependent on arms and ammunition which had been captured during the conflict with the British.

Through the minister for defence of Dáil Éireann and the chief-of-staff, the Provisional Government began to build a uniform fulltime nucleus of an army. Initially, recruitment was only from volunteers with previous experience: however, this was soon to extend to others. The British government transferred as much arms and equipment as was required. Churchill stated on 12 April 1922 that 4,000 rifles, 2,000 revolvers, 6 machine guns and ammunition had been handed over and that authority would be given for any further issue that may be required.[9]

Despite the fact that there was division there was no great bitterness between officers and men who took opposing sides. As always, the hope of a settlement existed. The possibility of re-uniting the army was one of the first matters considered by the Executive. Liam Lynch basically believed a settlement was possible through negotiations. Liam Mellows, secretary to the Executive, sent a letter on 14 April to the secretary of Dáil Éireann setting out their terms. This received no response. Lynch was opposed to any idea of a dictatorship. He wrote to his brother:

> In the past I made the most of any situation which arose, whether granted by the enemy or by any section in Ireland. I will do my best at the elections to keep Ireland from handing away the Republic or the least portion of her birthright. If we fail at the election I hope to have the army united under an Executive and not giving allegiance to any party or government ... If the army stands together – which I hope it will – we can save the country and the Republic. If we can force the Treaty party to draw up a Republican Constitution we are A1 again. This I consider quite possible.[10]

Lynch had fought bravely against the British, therefore the last thing he wanted was to fight against his own people. Above all else he passionately wanted to avoid Civil War. The conflict which was stirring, troubled him. He expressed this turmoil in his correspondence and also his belief that the constitution, when it would emerge, would be one which Republicans would accept; it would be a constitution under which a united army could serve without betraying its allegiance to the Republic.

Unfortunately neither the Executive nor Beggars Bush staff were in complete control of their respective forces throughout the country. Eight people had been killed and forty-nine wounded in armed clashes, and though no one wanted a Civil War the conflict was rapidly gaining momentum.[11]

A variety of problems loomed for the Executive which did not appear to be functioning as an effective unit. Other projects intruded, orders were given, sometimes without Lynch's knowledge. The fabric of authority was weakening.

Efforts for army unity

Since the early months of 1922 IRB conferences had been held in Dublin in an effort to save the organisation from disruption on the issue of the treaty. These conferences, called by the supreme council, comprised members of that body, together with the division and county centres of the entire organisation. At these conferences, the first of which took place on 10 January 1922, a large majority of the members were in favour of the treaty, but both views of the issue were debated with restraint and commendable objectivity.

Liam Lynch and Michael Collins were the principal protagonists of the two opposing viewpoints at these conferences, each respecting the others' apparent immovable position. Because of a sense of brotherhood, born out of their intimate association during the great national struggle of the past years, words of bitterness and anger were held in check. They both wanted, above all, to work together; but they failed. It was a failure for two great men who loved Ireland: a failure, which brought about catastrophe and sadness and led to the death of both men.

On 18 March the same IRB body met again, this time beneath the shadow of the cabinet's prohibition on the holding of the army convention, and in the knowledge that the convention would be held despite the ban. Michael Collins bore a large share of the responsibility for the cabinet's decision, and Liam Lynch a great share of the responsibility for the action which caused the convention to be prohibited: despite this, the two men met again in an atmosphere which, although strained, was still dominated by the spirit of the organisation. Both men, to a large extent, wielded power but neither could arrest disaster.

Collins had decided to accept the treaty and all that it entailed. Lynch had decided that, whether or not the people accepted the treaty, the army would not be committed to it, thereby holding a stance, under an Executive, until a constitution was drafted which would enable them to continue in allegiance to the Republic, when it could be truly called a Republic.

The second conference had adjourned without taking any decisions other than that the same body should meet again a month later. At the conference, which met on 19 April, the two chiefs-of-staff (of both divisions of the army) Lynch and Mulcahy, sat together. The chairman asked each individual for his views as to whether the position had changed in any material way since the previous meeting. Because of the deteriorating situation, which existed throughout the country, heated exchanges erupted between some of those present. The meeting was tense and explosive. Collins was extremely calm. According to him, the only suggestion the supreme council had to put before the meeting was that a committee should be appointed by the meeting to consider the constitution which would be available in three to four weeks. This committee, would in turn, report to the supreme council and summon a further meeting to discuss the constitution. Liam Lynch immediately rejected this suggestion. 'What was the point in waiting for three weeks for a Constitution which might not alter the position in any way?' He would have to take action, he said, unless there was a guarantee that the constitution would be a Republican one. Florence O'Donoghue suggested the appointment of a committee of six, three from each side, pro-treaty and anti-treaty, and this committee would try to find a basis of army reunification and report back to a further meeting. Agreement was reached on this point. (Diarmuid O'Hegarty, Florence O'Donoghue, Seán Ó Murthille, Martin Conlon, Liam Lynch and Joe McKelvey formed the committee.)

When the committee met the following day at 41 Parnell Square a suggestion was put forward that a truce between the two sections in the army would help towards reunification. Lynch, however, expressed the view that unless an overall basis of agreement could be found, a truce would be of little service. He held the view that any basis for unity should embrace all the national organisations such as the IRB, the army, Sinn Féin. His belief

118

was that an acceptable solution would require the bodies to reunite in allegiance to the existing Republic and reject the treaty. Being a realist, he had little hope of such a solution, but he still sought a way of avoiding Civil War.

This committee held four subsequent meetings, and these were ineffectual. Neither the constitution nor an indication of draft proposals was submitted. The proposal of pro-treaty nominees (Diarmuid O'Hegarty, Seán Ó Murthille, Liam Tobin, Martin Conlon) was rejected by Liam Lynch on the basis that being a secret organisation (IRB) these pro-treaty nominees could not act on behalf of that army with any binding authority.

At a further meeting it was agreed that it would serve no useful purpose to have prominent officers from both sides meet until a constitution was drawn up and the suggestion was made that hostilities on both sides be suspended. However, Lynch was adamant that, without guarantees, he could not wait a fortnight for a constitution: the wait had already been too long, he contended, and it was now time for action. He said that events were gaining momentum in the south, which needed immediate attention. Further, he asked for a guarantee from the other side that, within two days, they would maintain the independence of Ireland and produce a Republican constitution: the continuance of these meetings in the absence of a constitution was, he said, worthless. The maintenance of the Republic was of vital importance, and the Free State should not be allowed come into existence.

Throughout the country other groups sought some common ground in an effort to unite both sides. Officers who had taken an active part in the War of Independence and who were now on opposite sides held meetings in an effort to prevent a split. Dan Breen presided over many conferences. On the evening of 1 May, following a series of conferences on the last days of April, ten officers, five from each side, met and agreed to sign a document which stated that in order to 'avert this catastrophe we believe that a closing of the ranks all round is necessary.'[1] The document

119

further suggested army unification on the basis 'that the majority of the people of Ireland were willing to accept the treaty', conse-quently there should be 'an agreed election' with a view to form-ing an acceptable government.[2] Liam Lynch was, at this stage, beginning to distrust all efforts for reunification of the army as his only concern was 'the maintenance of the Republic'.

Subsequent to this agreed document, the army council issued a statement from the Four Courts, now Republican headquarters, expressing the opinion that:

> Attempts to make 'deals' with individual soldiers cannot result in unity; they can only intensify existing disunion ... The Executive elected by the army has the duty imposed on it ... it will deal with all efforts to reach unity, but it must be realised that unity cannot be bought at the expense of honour and principle.

On 3 May a deputation of five officers, representing the signa-tories of the appeal for unity, was admitted to Dáil Éireann. Seán O'Hegarty, on their behalf, addressed an assembly which, though divided on the treaty issue, was still strongly Republican in senti-ment. It was an appeal for a solution to avert a Civil War, which was now threatening the country. This led to the appointment by Dáil Éireann of a committee of ten in an effort to find a basis for unity.[3]

At 1.25 on 4 May the following statement was issued: 'A truce is declared on and from 4 p.m. today until 4 p.m. on Mon-day next with a view to giving both sections of the army an im-mediate opportunity of discovering a basis for army unification' [which were listed under three headings and signed by Liam Lynch and Owen O'Duffy].[4]

On 8 May a joint statement, signed by Liam Lynch and Owen O'Duffy, ordered a continuation of the truce indefinitely 'with a view to allow the army and Dáil committees to bring their work to completion'.[5]

The joint committee which had been formed on 4 May (con-sisting of Liam Lynch, Liam Mellows, Seán Moylan, Rory O'Connor, Séamus Robinson, Michael Collins, Richard Mulcahy, Diarmuid O'Hegarty, Owen O'Duffy, Gearóid O'Sullivan and Seán Mac Eoin) reached an agreement that all prisoners held by both sides who had not been charged with civil offences should be released forthwith and that buildings in Dublin, other than the Four Courts, occupied by Republicans, should be evacuated. In allowing the Four Courts to continue to be held, Lynch felt that there was a consensus of agreement, therefore he hoped that an accepted settlement would be reached.

'There can be unity if all forces will uphold the established Republic now as in the past,' he wrote in a letter to his godmother, Hannah Cleary. He said that the sacrifices of the past few years would be in vain if the Free State was accepted. 'At the moment I have hopes that the pro-treaty people have seen the error of their ways and that they will come to terms that will not let down the Republic. However, we cannot go back to a recurrence of last week, as some other way than Civil War must be found.'

A joint signed statement by Lynch and O'Duffy ordered the continuation of the truce, 'both sides to co-operate to maintain order to prevent acts of aggression against person or property'.

A letter dated 8 May to Lynch in the Four Courts from the Third Northern Division speaks 'from our point of view' in the north 'war conditions exist at GHQ. I consider it is up to you to issue orders to your following to fall in line with the majority and to fight under one command ... I would like the Chief-of-Staff and yourself to visit the Third Northern' as 'the army split is having a detrimental effect in the North ...'[6] The ten-member committee, following their approach to Dáil Éireann on 10 May, reported that there were two points on which they had reached agreement.

In summary:

(1) All legislators, Executive and judicial authority in Ireland, is and shall be, derived solely from the people of Ireland;
(2) That Dáil Éireann is a supreme governing authority in Ireland.

However, they did not find any basis of national unity, because according to Richard Mulcahy, 'our document ignored cause of split in army which they allege is the Treaty ...'[7]

The full reports on other points such as those dealing with elections were read to the Dáil. Dáil Éireann cabinet requested that the committees make a further effort towards unity. It was evident from the reports, which were debated in the Dáil on 17 May that an effort was being made to find some means of bridging the gap, which had been created since the treaty debates. Dáil Éireann cabinet requested that De Valera and Collins should re-examine the proposal. The two men sat in conference on 18 and 19 May at University College, Dublin, and on the afternoon of 20 May, they reached agreement and signed the Pact. The nation greeted the news with profound relief.

There was now a new incentive for Lynch and the army negotiators to continue their task of building on a sound base. The Pact would provide for the creation of a coalition parliament and government in which both pro-treaty and anti-treaty elements would be represented in proportion to their existing strength. During the weeks that followed, negotiations for army unity continued with Liam at the forefront of these negotiations. Proposals and counter-proposals were discussed, and various drafts and amendments drawn up until eventually in the first week of June documents were submitted by Liam Lynch and Seán Moylan.[8] Lynch, in his memorandum, called for the maintenance of an Irish Republic under the auspices of the government of the Republic; the IRA as the army 'under the control of an independent Executive'; both these bodies would maintain a working agreement. This broadly represented the negotiating position initiated by Lynch along army Executive lines.[9]

Seán Moylan in his ten proposals, listed a number of procedures, among them the 're-organisation staff' to be appointed under Liam Lynch, as deputy chief-of-staff, to re-organise the army 'with instructions that all inefficient officers be dispensed with.'

A third document of general army proposals and the personnel of the proposed army council and GHQ staff was put forward by the pro-treaty representatives (Collins, Mulcahy and O'Duffy) which dealt with appointments and general duties and activities within the army. In the 'Final Proposals for Agreement' members of an army council including Liam Lynch as deputy chief-of-staff were listed and were to be 'specially charged with re-organisation'.[10]

During these prolonged negotiations both sides had made considerable efforts to meet the others' viewpoint. Representatives of the pro-treaty view had conceded the right of the army to hold periodic conventions, with the freedom to elect an army council. Of the six principal members of the GHQ staff, three would have been pro-treaty and three anti-treaty. As Eoin O'Duffy had tendered his resignation on 22 May to become commissioner of the garda síochána, Liam Lynch would then succeed him as chief-of-staff and Liam Deasy as deputy.[11] Indeed, this position was favoured by Collins according to Liam Deasy, who believed that Collins would have liked to see Lynch as chief-of-staff.

Of the five principal staff officers of the army council three were to be anti-treaty and two pro-treaty. After long and anxious consideration, Liam Lynch accepted this basis of settlement. Indeed negotiations had gone into deadlock previous to the signing of the Pact, but the introduction of the Pact meant that parliament and government would derive their authority directly from the votes of the people, as happened in the first and second Dáil. This arrangement ultimately led to Lynch's acceptance of the final proposals for army council agreement.[12]

He wrote to his brother:

Come what may the Republic must still live. Even if the people and a small percentage of the army are against us for the time being, days or at least weeks will justify our actions when the Irish people can again come forward, standing erect before all the nations of the earth.[13]

Arms exchanged in northern offensive

In the northern counties of Antrim, Armagh, Down, Derry, Fermanagh and Tyrone, the election of May 1921 showed that of fifty-two seats in the whole area unionists secured forty, Republicans six and nationalists six. This illustrated that a minority of the population was Republican. However, the IRA, unknown to their compatriots in the rest of Ireland, continued under great difficulties to fight the British occupation forces. The material and moral support that was given by the majority of people in the rest of the country was lacking in this northern region. Despite handicaps, difficulties, and limitations, the IRA army units in these counties fought with strength and efficiency.

A 'Northern government' for the six counties came into existence as a result of an act passed by the British parliament on 23 December 1920 and the elections held under it on 24 May 1921. The act also provided for a 'Southern Parliament' for the remainder of the country and for a council of Ireland composed of an equal number of representatives from each area. Lloyd George and his government set up a unionist and Orange authority for the six counties which, determined to liquidate the IRA, proved to be even more unyielding than the British. The truce brought no more than a temporary cessation to hostilities. In the early months of 1922, Sir Henry Wilson was engaged as military advisor in the six counties. In March a Special Powers Bill was enacted which imposed the death penalty for possession of arms, authorised flogging for certain offences, enabled trial by jury to be suspended and coroner's inquests to be abolished.

The Ulster Special Constabulary, 'A', 'B' and 'C' classes, was rapidly expanding. Added to this were thirteen British battalions in the Royal Ulster Constabulary police. From early 1922 a policy of terrorism was implemented against Catholics and nationalists; burnings, lootings and evictions were the order of the day. (In the two years which ended in June 1922, 23,000 persons had been driven out, nearly 500 had been killed and over 1,500 wounded.) Liam Lynch and other members of the army were aware of the policy of terrorism even before the split in the army on the treaty issue. Army policy was that men and material from other areas should reinforce the Northern Division and that the northern minority should be aided to fight back against the forces engaged in such lawlessness. Even after the army split both sides had a common policy which they continued to operate jointly, though two separate army commands had been set up.

From documents available, the indications are that Collins was extremely anxious to work with Lynch on 'the Northern issue'. He knew that Lynch had the military experience as well as an overall view of the capabilities of the men in the Southern Division.

Lynch and Barry, in the Cork brigades, had found kidnapping a successful weapon at vital periods during the War of Independence; now during this intermediary period, this weapon was again used. When Collins failed to secure a reprieve for three IRA men due to be hanged in Derry jail and the release of Dan Hogan and his staff at Monaghan, IRA units under the command of Seán Mac Eoin, kidnapped forty-two loyalists and took them across the border as hostages. This operation, first outlined by Lynch[1] and sanctioned by Collins was successful.[2] Hogan was released, the Derry men were reprieved, and the hostages were returned unharmed.

The offensive, which began in Belfast on 18 May 1922, included men from the Southern Division. Whether reports of the results came to GHQ or to the IRA Executive, views were exchanged by both sections of the army. Lynch and Deasy liaised on the one side and Collins, Mulcahy, and O'Duffy on the other.[3]

Private negotiations for army unity, as well as decisions on the north, were on-going between Lynch and GHQ at Beggars Bush. According to a memo by the deputy chief-of-staff at GHQ, J. J. (Ginger) O'Connell, Liam Lynch was a constant visitor 'and was on better terms with the rest of GHQ staff than were O'Connell himself of Official Emmet Dalton.' Lynch's membership of the supreme council of the IRB was the co-ordinating link between Michael Collins, the president of that council, and other leading members – Mulcahy and O'Duffy.[4]

Lynch and Collins took a leading part in the formulation and operation of the measures agreed upon. It was decided to send a number of experienced officers from Lynch's division to the north to take charge of some of the divisions there, and to co-operate in activities against the forces of the northern government. Seán Lehane, Charlie Daly, Maurice Donnegan, Seán Fitzgerald and Séamus Cotter were appointed brigade commanders; other officers from the First Southern Division numbering about twenty were included in the party. Machine gunners were to follow. The operation was to take place from the Northern and Midland Divisions, which were outside the six county border. Donegal in the west would co-operate with Frank Aiken's division in Louth and Armagh, in the south-east. Their task was to make war on the crown forces in the north both on, and inside, the border.

Both sides of the army in the northern operation co-operated, but the pro-treatyites (Collins, Mulcahy, O'Duffy and Beggars Bush section) insisted that rifles or other weapons transferred to the Provisional Government by the British would not be taken into action, because these could be identified and might create embarrassment. These weapons were meant only to suppress the anti-treatyites. Arrangements were therefore made whereby Cork brigades supplied an agreed number of rifles towards the northern operation. Beggars Bush replaced these by handing back an equal number of British supplied weapons, in return. Most of the arms for the north came from the First and Second Southern Divisions.

Liam Deasy recollects, 'Liam Lynch, Seán Lehane and I went to the Four Courts on 15 April to arrange an exchange of rifles from the Cork brigades which were to be sent north to the areas along the border. These were to be exchanged for British rifles which had been supplied to the Free State army and which would be forwarded to the Cork brigade. This was one of many such exchanges which was secretly carried out through the mutual co-operation of both sections of the army, though there were problems with some reaching their proposed destination; Collins and Mulcahy were deeply implicated with us in these transactions.'

Before the signing of the treaty, Seán MacBride had been involved in the arrangement of a shipment of arms from Germany; following the signing, he asked Collins if there was to be any change of policy, but was told to carry on as before. This was done; a few shipments came into Waterford following which there was a considerable amount of collaborating between Collins and Lynch and the other Four Courts men. 'We were aware that arms were being transferred between the Four Courts and Beggars Bush. The result of the exchange was that arms were sent to Charlie Daly, Seán Lehane and others in Donegal. This was done to impede the new six county government and also as an aid to the Catholic minority. I believe Collins was genuine as was Lynch in this collaboration.'[5]

Pax O'Faolain recalls that in the summer of 1921, Charlie McGuinness was in charge of a cargo of arms due to land off Helvick Head, but, it appears that as a result of British intelligence, the ship and its cargo were seized. Bob Briscoe and Seán MacBride were in continuous negotiations for further arms' shipments from Germany. On 11 November 1921, the *Frieda* arrived off Helvick and lorries were on the spot to transport the contents of the cargo which consisted 'principally of Peter the Painters, parabellums, rifles and ammunition.'

MacBride and Briscoe negotiated and organised a further arms shipment, which was brought into Ballynagaul on 2 April 1922. This cargo, according to Pax O'Faolain, 'consisted of boxes of ammunition, rifles and parabellums – about six tons.' The collection supervised by Dick Barrett and received by Dan Gleeson and Seán Gaynor were 'transferred in vans northwards. Under

127

the arrangements between Collins and Lynch — we imported guns and we sent them to the north. Had we been preparing for a Civil War we would have held them here.'[6]

It is ironic that while the British government were sending arms and ammunition to Beggars Bush, with Collins' acknowledgement that they were to be used to quell the men under Lynch's command, Frank Fitzgerald, with Lynch's approval, was making arrangements with arms' dealers in London to secure arms which would be exchanged for those sent by the British government (10,000 rifles, 2,000 revolvers, 5 machine guns, 80 tons of bomb-making chemicals).[7]

Vigorous retaliation against the activities of the crown forces in the north, as agreed by both sides of the army, involved the risk of British re-occupation of the whole country and a renewed struggle with possible dire consequences – but that was a risk Lynch and the anti-treatyites were prepared to take. Disastrous though this might have seemed, Liam Lynch preferred it to the alternative of Civil War. No doubt Michael Collins felt this too. For both of them it was very evident that the project of mutual co-operation and brotherhood, mutually striking at a common enemy was far more desirable than were the heartaches of bringing their own people together during convention. 'They had, each for the other, a regard that went deeper than friendly comradeship – these two men that Ireland could so ill-afford to lose who were soon to die tragically on opposite sides in a war of brothers.'[8]

Although these two men had a common policy with regard to the six county area it was difficult to keep that policy isolated from the predominant issue which divided the entire country and the army. In the *Irish Independent* on 26 April 1922 Eoin O'Duffy made an inaccurate reference to the arms. Lynch's reply on the following day shows how confused transactions of the time were and how close the country was to Civil War:

> With reference to the alleged holding up of arms intended for the northern areas, these are the facts. The C/S and A/G phoned me to forward 30 Thompson guns, 10,000 rounds .303 and also 100 rifles,

these latter to be exchanged as soon as could be arranged. The following supplies of arms and ammunition were forwarded within 36 hours; 30 Thompson guns, 8,000 rounds of ammunition for T.M. Guns, 10,000 rounds .303, 75 rifles.

I also sent ten machine-gunners. Any of these supplied, I afterwards learned, did not get to the north, and the gunners after being detained for a week or so at Beggars Bush, were ordered home to their own areas after all being so urgently required by phone for the north. It is very easy to judge where the responsibility lies for the situation which now exists.

A general attack on the crowned forces in the six county area was planned in which units of the Fifth Northern and First Midland divisions were to participate. Columns were to be formed, the members of which would remain on continuous active service, and they would be maintained out of funds provided by Beggars Bush headquarters. Five hundred men were sent from the Second and Fourth Northern Divisions to the Curragh on an intensive two weeks training course: however Civil War intervened and the Curragh training dragged out to three months.

Frank Aiken had endeavoured from the outset to keep his division, the Third Northern, united in any decisions it might make on the question of the treaty. This unity of policy was what Lynch had also hoped for in the Southern Division.

On 18 April, Liam wrote to his brother Tom from GHQ in the Four Courts, 'not knowing the hour we will be attacked by machine-gun or artillery,'[9] and a few weeks later, as the situation developed, he wrote that he was 'absolutely convinced of wiping out the supposed Free State; but we don't mind giving it a slow death, especially when it means the avoidance of loss of life and general Civil War. If we are forced to it we will concentrate all our forces to wipe it out.'[10]

As time progressed it was becoming obvious to Dalton and O'Connell that they would eventually have to fight Lynch.[11]

A crisis developed on 7 June 1922 when Lynch and Mulcahy came together in a final attempt to avert a Civil War. Mulcahy and O'Duffy compromised by withdrawing troops from both Limerick and Templemore, J. J. O'Connell (deputy chief-of-staff, Beggars Bush) saw this 'as part of their general policy of conciliating Lynch.'[12] A series of prolonged negotiations were in progress during May and early June with both parties conceding points in an effort to reach a consensus on army reunification. On 12 May 1922 Lynch wrote to General O'Duffy:

> Since the Truce was declared no satisfactory effort has been made to discover a basis for army unification. Progress is impeded by officers on committee on your side not being willing to discuss the vital matters at issue. I must now request you to attend a meeting at 11 a.m. on Monday next the 15th instant at the Mansion House, after which negotiations must cease if a definite understanding for agreement is not reached.[13]

This meeting led to further proposals; a memorandum sent by Lynch on 4 June, suggesting the formation of an army council to uphold 'the maintenance of an Irish Republic ... with a working agreement ... between the government of the Republic and the Executive of the IRA.'[14] Richard Mulcahy, minister for defence sent a response on 12 June in which he outlined proposals for army reunification which allowed for 'a periodic Convention to elect an Army Council of seven', and that the minister for defence be appointed by the government, and the chief-of-staff to be appointed by the minister for defence.[15] In the Mulcahy papers there are several letters from Lynch dealing with this issue. Mulcahy notes 'the Four Courts representatives considered that the GHQ staff document ignored the cause of the split, which they alleged was the Treaty.'[16] Other correspondence demonstrate Lynch's insistence that the signing of the treaty created the army split.[17] Mulcahy appears to accept this. Lynch suggested that upon O'Duffy's resignation he himself would succeed him as chief-of-staff, with Liam Deasy as deputy. Florence O'Donoghue calls it an 'abnormal suggestion'. A document entitled 'Final Proposals for Agreement' from GHQ suggested staff re-organisation with 'deputy chief-of-staff – Liam Lynch – to be specially charged with re-organisation. Deputy chief-of-staff – Liam Deasy – in charge of training.'[18] (In this proposal it appears that there would be two anti-treaty men in the position of deputy chief-of-staff – one in change of re-organisation and the other on training.) The formulation of a war council of eight members would have given the anti-treaty side five representatives against three pro-treaty. (Of the six principal members of GHQ staff three would been pro-treaty and three anti-treaty, but it was expected that Eoin O'Duffy would become commissioner of the gárda siochána – on 22 May, he had tendered his resignation from post of chief-of-staff.)

O'Connell who held the position as deputy chief-of-staff at Beggars Bush totally disagreed with the plan formulated by Collins, Mulcahy and O'Duffy for reunification of the army under the Provisional Government.

Lynch, Deasy and Seán Moylan were in favour of the reunification proposals, but when the Executive met on 14 June the proposals were rejected, though a resolution was passed which stated that, 'No offensive will be taken against the Beggars Bush forces.'[19] Following this meeting Lynch wrote to the minister for defence and expressed the view that deputy chief-of-staff was not on, for the Executive:

> Personnel of GHQ of your 'Immediate proposals' are not acceptable. While the Political Agreement provided for a M/D representing the army we are agreeable to present M/D until sanctioned or otherwise by next Convention. Executive insists on C/S but are prepared to give Beggars Bush forces D/C/S, Q/M/General, Director/Publicity.[20]

The Four Courts Executive wanted Lynch to hold the position of chief-of-staff at GHQ in the proposed army reunification; they were prepared to have a Beggars Bush member as deputy rather than visa versa as suggested by Beggars Bush.

De Valera, at a later date, in an interview with the *Melbourne Irish News* said that Lynch had a suspicion that Beggars Bush 'were playing for time', but was hopeful of unification of both wings 'and the continuation of the army united as the army of the Republic ... The lengths to which he was prepared to go even made him to be suspected of a tendency to go too far by some of his comrades ...'[21]

Lynch was hopeful that under the Pact in a coalition agreement with a responsible government, the army situation could be resolved; however, the political situation now appeared to deteriorate. Griffith and Collins were summoned to London on 26 May 1922. Collins returned and signed, with De Valera, a joint appeal to the nation to observe the Pact. Collins again went to London on 13 June and on his return he travelled to Cork, making a speech on 14 June which was clearly in breach of the Pact.

The constitution, which had been long awaited, appeared in the press on the morning of Friday 16 June 1922, the day of the general election. It brought bitter disappointment to Republicans – included was the oath of allegiance to a British monarch and the constitution itself was made subject to the terms of the treaty. In addition, this copperfastened the 1920 Government of Ireland Act – a partitioned Ireland (six northern counties) as part of the British empire.

The hopes and expectations of Liam Lynch were sadly shattered. He wrote to his brother that night:

> Well, Tom, the situation generally is beyond anything I could any longer hold out hope for. As you often said, I always held out hope to the last, but really all are blighted now and as far as I am personally concerned I feel all my life's work has been in vain. Surely this is a terrible way to feel. Would we could even get back our glorious dead.[22]

Here was a note of despair! A shattered dream for a man who had tried, at all costs, to maintain some semblance of unity.

Meanwhile Ernie O'Malley pressed for the organisation of some contingency plans in case of war; Lynch reassured him as he had on a previous occasion, that negotiations would begin shortly and that there would be no need for any action. O'Malley then asked if he could inspect the defences of the Four Courts. Lynch consented. The following day, O'Malley, with Paddy

O'Brien (Liscarroll) made the inspection and outlined recommendations. He then drew up a report, which he forwarded to Lynch as C/S, but O'Malley said 'it was not acted upon'. While army negotiations continued, Liam Lynch ordered the Dublin brigade to evacuate some of the positions in the city 'in order to promote better understanding.'[23]

It was under the mantle of angry disappointment that the army delegates who had made up the previous convention assembled in Dublin on Sunday 18 June 1922. The explosive atmosphere, which had prevailed over the previous week, remained unabated making discussion of army reunification pointless. Extremely conscious of the imminence of Civil War, Liam Lynch requested that Florence O'Donoghue move for the adoption of the army proposals and so prolong the dreaded day. In an atmosphere of anger, disillusionment and bitterness, the motion for acceptance was debated. Despite the disturbed feelings of many of the delegates the debate was conducted with admirable restraint.

As the meeting proceeded Tom Barry proposed that instead of further discussion on the proposals for army reunification, the convention should consider a motion to resume war against the British forces in Ireland. (Only posts in Dublin and the six counties were then occupied by foreign troops.) This motion was opposed, not only by Liam Lynch and Cathal Brugha, but by practically all the delegates from the First Southern Division and by many others; however, it was supported by members of the Executive opposed to the reunification proposals. Lynch disagreed with Barry, and urged moderation, pointing out that such an action would be irresponsible. Both Barry and Lynch were strong-minded Republicans and spent some time arguing tactics instead of principles. Barry and his supporters believed that direct action would bring the pro-treaty soldiers in Beggars Bush and throughout the country back into a united front and that they could together fight the common enemy – Britain.

Though Seán MacBride agreed in principle with the proposal he said, 'it was very foolish of Barry to have put forward such a resolution at the convention. It was neither the time nor the place for it. In fact it put the onus of declaring war on Great Britain, on a body of men who had been selected by various units of the army to select an Executive which was to appoint a chief-of-staff and to direct the policy of the army until a Republican Government was formed. I understand that Barry proposed that motion to counter-balance Liam Lynch's proposal and to avoid a repetition of such incidents. As a policy the substance of his motion was quite right, but by putting it forward at a Convention without consulting anybody as he did, he was putting those who supported that policy into a very awkward position.'[24]

At the meeting it became apparent from a speech made by Liam Mellows that there was a very big split in the Executive based on the fundamental decision of policy. Lynch, Moylan and Deasy were leading the opposition to Barry's motion and it became quite clear that once the motion was dealt with, a proposition would be made that the Republican army be united and controlled by the Free State army.

It appeared on the surface at least that the treaty was workable. Tom Barry was totally against this whole idea of being under Free State army control. However, sensing the mood he felt restrained; beyond proposing his motion, which he hoped would bring army unity, he made no attempt to justify it. Though Rory O'Connor and Liam Mellows saw Barry's mistake in bringing forward this motion as a proposal to the convention, without any previous discussion, they understood that this was the only policy that could be consistently followed by the anti-treatyites. An air of depression and solemnity permeated this convention. Barry's motion was passed by a couple of votes but was challenged on the grounds that a brigade was present which was not represented at the last convention. Following discussion, the objection was upheld: a fresh vote was taken giving the result 103 for the motion, 118 against. Some heated discussion on the compromise proposals followed, and Lynch declared that he would no longer go on as chief-of-staff.

Twelve members of the Executive who had voted with Barry chose Joseph McKelvey, to replace Liam Lynch, as their new chief-of-staff.

Barry and Rory O'Connor would not accept the continued delay. They left the room, followed by their supporters, announcing that they were returning to the Four Courts. Seán MacBride had the difficult task of announcing that a further convention would be held in the Four Courts the following morning. 'There was an absolute silence and I could hear my steps like shots from the top of the room to the door.'[25] A few more delegates left; the Executive was now split; the anti-treaty section of the army was split; the convention broke up in gloom and confusion. A division had come about not on reunification proposals, but on the question of resumption of war with Britain.

The state of the army was chaotic during the ten days which followed this third convention. As the proposals for reunification had not been voted upon, Lynch hoped that reunification was still not dead; however, without the coalition government (Collins/De Valera Pact), there did not seem to be any prospect of acceptance by the majority of the anti-treatyites in the army. If a vote for army reunification proposals had been taken would the outcome have been different? Events were gaining momentum; by this time the political atmosphere created by the treaty division was now cemented by the rejection of the Pact.

Disunity and Civil War

Following the unveiling on 22 June 1922 of a memorial to railway men killed in the First World War, Field Marshal Sir Henry Wilson, military advisor to the six county administration, was assassinated in London. Commandant Reginald Dunne and Volunteer Joseph O'Sullivan of the IRA London's battalion were arrested. There was no doubt in the minds of the British ministers that the Four Courts garrison was to blame for the killing. This was not so. Whether or not an earlier order given by Michael Collins was never cancelled is still unclear. What is clear is that Dunne and O'Sullivan were acting upon orders which they accepted as official and therefore legitimate. (Subsequently the two men were hanged.) On 24 June, Macready, still in command of the remnant of British forces in Dublin, received orders to attack the Four Courts the following day.[1]

While preparing to carry out orders the British cabinet altered its decision, cancelled its instructions and instead sent an ultimatum to the Provisional Government on 26 June demanding that the occupation of the Four Courts be brought to an end. Meanwhile, the Four Courts garrison continued to commandeer vehicles and arms from the remaining British troops. The Provisional Government was being criticised by Churchill and other members of the British government for making no move against these attacks. The entire strength of the Republican movement in Ireland could perhaps have been mobilised, had there been a call to close the ranks. The Pact had not been observed and the Dáil was to re-assemble on 30 June. There was no call for reunification of the army against the threat of British demands. Instead, things moved swiftly and inevitably to a climax. Pro-treaty deputy chief-of-staff, J. J. (Ginger) O'Connell was arrested by Republican forces as a reprisal for the arrest of Commandant Leo Henderson who had been held by Provisional Government troops whilst engaged in commandeering transport for the removal of

Gen. Mulcahy, chief-of-staff of Provisional Government forces, inspecting members of the National Army at Collins Barracks after the evacuation of the British Forces in 1922
(Courtesy, Cork Public Museum)

Michael Collins	*Ernie O'Malley, staff captain of the*
Prior to the Civil War, during the	*IRA, organiser for Michael Collins,*
early months of 1922 Lynch, Collins	*involved in engagements with Liam*
and Mulcahy were in regular commu-	*Lynch in Cork No. 2 brigade, and*
nication – all three were IRB members	*with him as a member of the IRA*
	Executive

supplies to the north – a project on which both sides were still nominally co-operating. A swift movement against the divided anti-treaty forces could, it was thought, bring an end to hostilities. At 3.40 a.m. on 28 June 1922 the Provisional Government issued an ultimatum to the Four Courts garrison. This was refused. Within an hour the attack on the Four Courts opened.

General Dalton, director of military operations, urged the use of artillery to bombard the Four Courts. 'It was my belief that the using of these guns would have a demoralising effect on the garrison inside, that they would shortly surrender.'[2] Field guns, borrowed from the British forces, and supervised by British personnel, were used to shell the historic building. The Civil War had truly begun.

The shelling continued until noon on Friday 30 June. Fire had spread through most of the building by Friday morning and by mid-day the position had become untenable. Two of the garrison had been killed and a number wounded. Explosives which had been loaded on trucks for the north blew up and killed a number of pro-treaty forces.

The first prisoner of the Civil War was Tom Barry who tried to gain entrance disguised as a nurse. Other prisoners included Rory O'Connor, Liam Mellows, Joe McKelvey, Dick Barrett, Seán MacBride and Peadar O'Donnell.

Liam Lynch and a number of his officers were at the Clarence Hotel across the river from the Four Courts when the attack opened. Awakened by the eighteen pounders, they quickly assembled and, without hesitation, decided to support the men on whom the Provisional Government forces had opened attack. That decision by Lynch and his men brought the First Southern Division as well as other Republican units throughout the country into the conflict and ended any possibility that the aggressors might have had easy victory. The Provisional Government had miscalculated that there had never been a complete break between the majority of the Executive in the Four Courts and the minority in the Clarence Hotel. Earlier that week Lynch had spoken to O'Connor, Mellows, McKelvey and other members and they were still trying to work out a policy on which they could agree. Lynch had resumed his role as chief-of-staff on 27 June following a meeting in the Four Courts.[3]

A council of war of the officers in the Clarence issued a hurried proclamation calling on the army to resume the fight for the Republic; this was signed by the members of the Executive present. A decision was taken that the Southern Division officers return to their commands. Lynch would go south and set up headquarters in the country. Oscar Traynor was in command in Dublin. (He started to mobilise the Dublin brigade in support of the men in the Four Courts.)

On their way from the Clarence Hotel to Kingsbridge railway station when returning south Liam Lynch, Liam Deasy and Seán Culhane were halted by a party of Provisional Government troops under Liam Tobin and taken to Wellington barracks. Lynch and Deasy were interviewed separately by Eoin O'Duffy. 'You'd better be on your way south,' O'Duffy said, accompanying his parting words with a handshake.[4]

In the Provisional Government *War News* dated 22 July it was alleged that Lynch was released by O'Duffy because he said he gave his 'word of honour that he disapproved of the policy of irregulars and would not assist them.'

What Lynch had said to O'Duffy was, 'I think ye are all mad.'[5] Lynch and O'Duffy had always been good friends and had worked hand in hand during the long drawn out conferences for army re-unification; so it is understood that it was through goodwill O'Duffy had allowed Lynch to go free, believing that he would help limit the Civil War in the south. Upon release, Lynch, Deasy and Culhane joined the other southern officers at Kingsbridge. Séamus Robinson, who was going to Tipperary to raise some troops, chastised Lynch and Deasy for creating the division of which the Provisional Government had taken advantage. Lynch sternly replied, 'We are all together now', and tried to persuade Robinson not to return with forces to Dublin as Robinson had planned. Lynch then outlined a strategy in which the anti-treatyites would work together keeping the south united, so that finally the treatyites 'would succumb to the better force'. Robinson was determined to return to Dublin. They parted and went their separate ways.[6]

Lynch, Deasy and the others took a train which did not, however, go beyond Newbridge. Seán and Con Moylan went to Kilcullen where they procured a car and returned to pick up Lynch, Deasy, Culhane and Seán McSwiney. (A group which included Frank Barrett of Clare had got another car.) Lynch's party was held up at Castlecomer by a section of the Provisional Government troops under Captain Murphy. Seán Moylan bluffed his way out and obtained a supply of petrol and oil for the car. As they were about to resume their journey the officer courteously invited them to the barracks for a meal. Lynch declined and said he wanted to be on his way, but Deasy intervened and revealed that they had not eaten since early morning. Lynch then agreed. They were treated to a very substantial meal. The men talked freely about the war and spoke about the regretful conflict which had arisen since the signing of the treaty. According to Deasy, 'whatever tension had previously existed, quickly melted away'. Both sides of the group who sat around the table expressed a genuine hope that the conflict would not develop any further. It was past midnight as Lynch and his men rose to go, expressing their gratitude for the courtesy and generosity that had been extended to them. One of the officers then produced a large sheet of ruled foolscap, placed it on the table and invited the men to leave autographs as a token of friendship and as a souvenir of comrades in arms. Lynch, with Deasy and the other men, did so. There was a warm handshake and a salute from the guard, then both sides parted.

Lynch was very annoyed when, a few days later, the Provisional Government announced that Deasy and himself had assured O'Duffy that they were neutral, or at least that they would take no part in the war and that this was confirmed by their signatures as autographs in Castlecomer barracks.

In the *War News* it was alleged that Lynch, who had been released in Dublin by O'Duffy was later that day re-arrested at Castlecomer and again released, 'repeating to Col Prout that he would not take part in the fight'. This statement and that alleged to have been made to O'Duffy were untrue, and though no more than propaganda, they were unhelpful in the prevailing tense climate. Deasy maintained that this was a sad epilogue to a night when the military 'and ourselves fraternised so freely and parted in such a friendly manner'.[7]

That night, after Lynch and the others had left Castlecomer and joined the Cork/Dublin road at Urlingford, they were again stopped at Littleton, but, almost immediately, allowed to continue. At Cashel they were held up again, but there Tom Carnew, another old friend, gave them the all clear. They arrived at Mallow around 8.30 a.m. on 29 June. On this, the feast of SS Peter and Paul, they had breakfast and went to Mass. For the remainder of the day they engaged in a full stocktaking exercise, and Lynch summoned a meeting of those officers in the brigade who could be contacted. At this meeting there was unanimous agreement to organise forces on a war footing and to first capture Limerick city and so gain control of the Shannon crossing. It was Lynch's hope, according to Paddy O'Brien, 'that by isolating the south and cementing it, the Provisional Government forces could become frustrated and so relent their holding'.[8]

Lynch wrote to all units in order to state his exact position and also the course events were taking:

> Owing to statements to some newspapers and general false rumours amongst the army, I deem it necessary that all ranks should know at once the position of Army Command. It is not possible to give a full outline of situation until a more satisfactory army position prevails. Army Executive recently differed in the matter of policy which was brought about by the final proposal of Minister for Defence for army unification. As a result while remaining a member of Executive I have not carried on as C/S since Convention of 18th inst. Owing to attack on GHQ and other posts occupied by our troops by Dáil forces, and position created by draft Free State Constitution, I have again taken up duty as C/S since Thursday, 29th inst, with Temporary HQ at Mallow. Communications are established with all Southern, Western and Eastern Divisions, and a united plan of action being carried out. Assistant C/S has been detailed to command Dublin and Northern areas, and I am in constant communication with the latter. By this evening we hope to have made

rapid progress towards complete control of west and southern Ireland for the Republic. Latest reports from Dublin show that the Dublin brigade have control of situation and that reinforcements and supplies are being dispatched through their assistance.

I appeal to all men to maintain the same discipline as in recent hostilities, and not interfere with civilian population except absolute military necessity requires it.

Liam Lynch
Chief-of-Staff[9]

Compromise Limerick agreement

Six months of talks on the possibility of a Civil War had passed yet there appeared to be no concrete plans to conduct such a war. From the outset, the Executive was working from a disadvantageous position; four of their members were prisoners. (Tom Barry had been captured in an effort to get into the Four Courts during the fight. Liam Mellows, Rory O'Connor and Dick Barrett were taken after the surrender of the building.) Lynch's staff was totally inadequate.

Upon the evacuation of British forces throughout the country, Republicans had taken over most of the British posts and were practically in complete control of the country south of a line from Waterford to Limerick. The Provisional Government had the advantage of having a definite policy, control of the money and the ability to call on the British for war supplies. On 6 July 1922 they issued a call to arms which met with a ready response.

Two posts in the south, Skibbereen and Listowel, which were occupied by Provisional Government troops, were attacked and captured.

Connie Neenan said 'when our brigade in Cork heard of the attack on the Four Courts we went straight away to reinforce Limerick ... and got caught between two Free State posts. On the first night of that attack there was some shooting and Spillane fell and died within five minutes ... That was the start of it for us. We went from there to Rathkeale where we met Liam Lynch.'[1] They moved on to Adare, captured a post and then to Limerick and further fighting. 'We lost a few more of our men, among them Paddy Norton, Dear Christ but he was a terrific man at a time when we needed him.'[2]

Lynch was extremely disturbed by a late night report stating that Ashford Castle had been commandeered by Donnacha O'Hannigan: not alone were they neighbours but they were very close friends and had fought together during the War of Inde-

143

pendence. Lynch discussed the position with Deasy and his men. True, actual fighting had not yet begun, but it was evident to Lynch that O'Hannigan would be captured. There was no possible way he could escape, and as he was pro-treaty the situation was delicate. Lynch was in a quandary as he did not want to abuse his authority in favour of a personal friend. As a way out, Deasy suggested that he himself would go to Ashford and make some arrangements with the anti-treaty commander. Lynch welcomed the suggestion and gave Deasy full authority to act as he saw fit. Deasy cooled the situation and the local IRA commander allowed O'Hannigan to leave with his men bearing their arms.

It was the first touch of sadness in the conflict of friend against friend. 'When I returned to Mallow that night and told Lynch how the O'Hannigan affair had been solved, his happiness and satisfaction were very evident,' Deasy said. No matter what differences were to arise later, Lynch and Deasy decided that they would try to make every effort to end a campaign which they felt was going to destroy solidarity.

On the following day, 30 June, Lynch left for Limerick and with him were men from the Cork brigade led by Dan Sando O'Donovan – the first contingent to enter the city. On their way to Limerick they took Free State posts at Croom, Adare and Patrick's Well. They entered the city from the western end and occupied the new barracks as well as other strategic positions.

At the other end of the city they were opposed by the East Clare brigade under the command of Michael Brennan with men from Limerick city and county who had taken the pro-treaty side. Brennan and Lynch had worked closely during the War of Independence, often collaborating as in the kidnapping of Lucas, and they were now on opposing sides. Lynch told Deasy that he wished he could find common ground to settle the situation with men like Brennan, O'Hannigan and Michael Collins. 'The conflict was eating into his very soul, he did not want to oppose his friends, but at all times he wanted to do what was best for Ireland,' according to Liam Deasy. Lynch believed that 'if hostilities

144

could be avoided in the Munster area perhaps the situation might not deteriorate.'[3]

Michael Brennan of the Western Division said that, 'the holding of Limerick was the holding of the whole south and west'. Brennan, with the government forces, controlled an area which covered the whole of Clare, part of Galway and the Ballinasloe railway line – 'most of the men in these posts were unarmed'. It is obvious that Lynch realised this. Brennan was hoping for rifles which were to be sent from Dublin. 'My whole fright was that Lynch would attack me before the guns turned up, because we couldn't last. I had to keep him talking to keep him from attacking. We met and we met, altogether about a dozen times. We used to meet in the presbytery of the Augustinian church where we argued and argued.'

The fact that Lynch seemed to be totally in control of the south was, according to Brennan, 'painfully true'. Lynch was convinced, at this stage, that there was nothing to be gained by further bloodshed and that some agreement should be reached in order to control the situation. Brennan was under the impression that Lynch was really only bluffing, that all he wanted was a free hand to over-run the country and wreck the treaty and to impose his views on the people. But others, those who worked with him, claimed that 'Lynch genuinely wanted peace and made every effort to maintain some form of peace and to avoid the civil strife'.[4] During these early days of the struggle three men, Professor Alfred O'Rahilly, University College Cork, Frank Daly, managing director of Suttons and chairman of Cork Harbour Board and T. P. Dowdall, who supported the War of Independence, were anxious to meet Liam Lynch and explore any and every possibility that might lead to peace. The men arrived in Mallow and, having discussed the matter with Lynch and Deasy, they returned to Cork disappointed.

Lynch had thought that the take-over of Limerick would be a mere formality but this was not the case. He took over the new barracks where he established his headquarters and then occupied the Strand barracks, Castle barracks and Ordnance barracks. Shortly after Lynch's arrival in Limerick, Dan Breen and Stephen O'Mara intervened to avoid a conflict; at an arranged meeting, Donnacha O'Hannigan and Liam Lynch signed a truce by which both hoped a permanent settlement would follow.[5] The agreement was signed at 6.30 on 4 July 1922 which was to be put into effect by 12 o'clock that night.[6] The agreement, under nine points, listed the areas which should be occupied by both sides, and stated that such an agreement should be maintained until both sides of the army Executive forces and Beggars Bush – 'find a solution to the problem'.

In an earlier agreement with Liam Deasy, O'Hannigan had agreed to evacuate the First Southern Division area which was in the main anti-treaty: now Lynch undertook not to occupy any posts in O'Hannigan's old brigade area, East Limerick.

The agreement never came into operation because Commandant General D. A. MacMaghunsa (McManus) from GHQ wrote a letter to Liam Lynch the next day in which he stated that Commandant General Brennan and Commandant General O'Hannigan who had been discussing terms of agreement 'had no authority whatever to enter into such an agreement'. He went on to say that he reserved full liberty of action and had told these officers not to partake in a further meeting which had been arranged 'and that they are to have no further communication with you on the matter.' Despite this letter the two parties to the agreement came together next day, and, in the presence of two prominent priests, signed a new agreement at 1.30 a.m.on 7 July which stated that in the interests of 'a united Ireland and to save our country from utter destruction' it was agreed that as soon as Seán Mac Eoin could be brought into the area a meeting would be convened and would be attended by all the commandants of all the divisions in the south and west regions. It further stated 'that the forces now opposed to one another in Limerick city end for all time this fratricidal strife in view of the meeting of Divisional Commandants in Limerick. And as a guarantee of good faith towards a permanent agreement the Divisional Council of the First Western Division Dáil Forces IRA agree to hand in their resignations if agreement is not reached at the meeting of Divisional Commandants ...'

The agreement listed buildings which would be occupied by the opposing forces; it also stated that troops in Limerick city were not to appear in public with arms except by liaison arrangement and that 'a truce now exists between the Executive forces, Irish Republican Army and First Western Division and the Fourth Southern Division Dáil Forces Irish Republican Army until the Conference ends between the Divisional Commandants. All our posts to be withdrawn to the agreed centres by 6 o'clock Friday evening 7 July 1922.'

The agreement was signed by Liam Lynch, Donnacha O'Hannigan and Michael Brennan.

MacMaghunsa (McManus) wrote to Lynch that 'while absolutely disapproving of this agreement' he was willing to allow this matter to go ahead on condition that 'there is no change in the military position here' but he would not 'agree to any interference with our present strong military position', and would even forego using the advantages gained for the sake of national agreement.

It was Brennan's opinion that because of this agreement with Liam Lynch, Dublin was probably saved from invasion by the southern forces. There seems to be little doubt that Lynch was hoping for victory without bloodshed, and whether there was a flaw in the Lynch/O'Hannigan agreement or not, the fact that Brennan's name was added, and as Brennan and Lynch were understood to be loyal and sincere, it was felt that their signatures might at least encourage moderation. It was of course a time when communication was slow, when men's loyalties were torn and their emotions played upon, when men and women followed their leader rather than their own convictions; Lynch, in using his authority wisely, gained increased respect amongst his comrades and followers.

Unfortunately, this effort to prevent even a portion of the country from the scourge of Civil War failed because the men who controlled Provisional Government policy decided to destroy that section of the army which refused to accept the treaty. A meeting of both sides of the divisional commandants in the south did not find favour in Dublin. Two officers, one from each side, were detailed to go to Dublin to convey the proposals to the Provisional Government. Seán, McCarthy (instructed by Lynch on behalf of the anti-treatyites) went, but his opposite number was never appointed, so the project fell through, consequently for a few days an uneasy peace reigned in Limerick. Then at 5.30 on the evening of 7 July the Provisional Government forces at William Street opened fire on the Ordnance barracks and the pattern of the conflict in Dublin was repeated. The Limerick/ Waterford line which ran through Tipperary, Golden, Cashel, Fethard, Clonmel and Carrick-on-Suir held for a short time, but the lack of artillery and machine-guns eventually meant surrender.

Lynch moved his headquarters from Limerick to Clonmel on 11 July, and on 13 July was joined by Éamon de Valera who was assigned by Lynch to a post on the staff of the director of operations. De Valera hoped for peace which would include some form of compromise. When Robert Brennan and Erskine Childers arrived next day they found Lynch pinning flags to a wall map along 'the Waterford/Limerick Line' and De Valera urging a settlement 'while they still had something to give away'.

On 4 July 1922 Frank Aiken had written to the minister for defence (Richard Mulcahy) intimating that he would not fight on either side because in his view a 'fight would only ruin the country without gaining any grounds for the Republic.' He went south and saw Liam Lynch. Unable to make any impression on Lynch's fixed conviction (that defence of the Republic in arms was the only means left of preventing its extinction) he left him and returned to Dublin to inform the minister for defence of his decision. Next morning the barracks at Dundalk was captured by

Provisional Government forces, Aiken was taken prisoner but was given parole. He went to Dublin again for another interview with the minister for defence but was re-arrested on returning to Dundalk. He escaped and went on to fight with the Republican forces and to take the stand outlined by Liam Lynch.

Again on 15 July Lynch moved his headquarters to Fermoy barracks. De Valera went with Lynch but shortly afterwards returned to Clonmel to work with Séamus Robinson O/C Second Southern Division, in an effort to reinforce the Limerick/Waterford line, which they thought should be held.

Meanwhile at a Provisional Government meeting on Wednesday 12 July, a Council of War was held. Michael Collins announced that he had arranged to take up duty as commander-in-chief of the army and would not until further notice be able to act in his ministerial capacity. W. T. Cosgrave was appointed to act as chairman of the Provisional Government and as minister for finance 'in the absence of Mr Collins on military duty'.[7]

Richard Mulcahy was made chief-of-general-staff (he also held on to his post as minister for defence) as Eoin O'Duffy had the task of general-in-charge of the South-western Division. This cancelled any hope, which Lynch had of maintaining stability in the south and the west.

The treatyites captured Limerick on 20 July and took advantage of the large coastal area with convenient ports at strategic points. The landing of troops took place first in Waterford on 23 July and during the following days Provisional Government troops landed in Westport and then advanced to Castlebar. Ernie O'Malley wrote to Lynch on 21 July, 'Could you give me an outline of your military and national policy, as we are in the dark here.' Lynch's reply stated his aim was 'to maintain the existing Republic' and that this would be by means of guerrilla warfare.[8] On 26 July Roderick Connolly, president of the communist party visited Lynch in Fermoy. That day a train had been wrecked at Kingsbridge and workers refused to repair it. Connolly proposed that a Republican government should be set up with Cork city as its capital and, 'that a democratic programme should be published to rally the people, and that in this way the Republic should be saved.'[9] Lynch was unimpressed. He reported the incident to a staff meeting the next day and then dismissed the matter.

Provisional Government (treatyite) forces took Tipperary town on 30 July. On that same day, Harry Boland was shot by armed men who burst into his hotel in Skerries; he died two days later. Carrick-on-Suir was captured by treatyite forces on 2 August, Kilmallock on 5 August and Clonmel on 8 August. On 2 August troops landed in Fenit. From there they pushed on to Tralee and during the following days, they occupied Castleisland, Listowel and Farranfore. Limerick was already in their hands. On 8 August the landing at Passage West, though vigorously opposed by Republicans, opened the way for occupation of Cork. Other landings at Youghal, Glandore, and Kenmare laid most of Cork open to occupation by Provisional Government forces. Though larger towns and villages were occupied, substantial areas of the country still remained in Republican hands. It was a return to the old type guerrilla warfare, a warfare with which many of the Republicans and Provisional Government forces were not unfamiliar.

During the first month of the war over 1,000 Republican prisoners were taken. It was now a 'war of brothers' where friends fought against friends, neighbours against neighbours and brothers against brothers: the civilian population were no longer behind those who wanted to continue to fight. On 10 August 1922, Lynch wrote to Ernie O'Malley requesting a daily report:

> Do your utmost to order doing of line and wires and also all road communications. Limerick agreement means O'Hannigan and Brennan divisions are adopting neutral attitude. This is glorious if they stand by their signatories.
> God bless our arms.[10]

After the occupation of Waterford the line from there to Limerick was subjected to pressure at many points. Golden was taken by treatyite forces in a surprise attack; they took Carrick-on-Suir after a three-day struggle and Republicans had to evacuate Tipperary. Broken at many points, the Republican line collapsed. The O'Hannigan/Brennan/Lynch agreement was overturned. The forces defending the line formed into columns and unsuccessfully began to harass the garrisons.

On 11 August Lynch evacuated Fermoy barracks and burned it. This was the last post to be held by Republican forces. It was a sad Liam Lynch who took his personal belongings and valuable papers to walk out into the streets where he had issued his first challenge to the British military almost three years earlier. Once more the Chief of the IRA was without barracks, base stores, or supply service. Siobhán (Creedon) Langford recalls being with Liam and his men as they evacuated:

> A group of officers stood with Liam Lynch in the barrack square It was a heart-breaking moment. Suddenly Dan Mulvihill's fine voice rang out in the popular aria from Verdi's *Ill Travatore*, 'Home to our Mountains'. Appreciation of Dan's performance flashed on every face, and the dejection of the hour was somewhat lightened.

As Liam Lynch looked back at the burning building he pondered and asked what would the next chapter be for him. He did not expect an answer. The first phase of the Civil War had ended and a new one was about to begin.[11]

Jerry MacEvilly (Cork No. 2 brigade) in Fermoy barracks, Feb. 1922. (Republicans took Fermoy barracks upon British evacuation. Liam Lynch used these premises as headquarters until 11 Aug. 1922.) In 1921, Jerry MacEvilly in Con Leddy's unit captured Moorepark from the British military. In October 1922 while fighting with Republican forces, MacEvilly was arrested in Araglin, interned, in Hare Park, the Curragh, until 21 Dec. 1923
(Courtesy, Michael MacEvilly)

Memo on Michael Collins' death

After the evacuation of Fermoy on 11 August 1922 the adjutant general, Con Moloney, had established headquarters in the Glen of Aherlow. He also acted as adjutant to the Southern Command. (Both headquarters were in the Glen but Lynch did not move into that area until 25 September.) The change over to guerrilla warfare cost the Republican forces time and effort and produced a series of new problems. Morale, which had been high during the fight against the British, was now considerably set back. Peace negotiations were formulated by persons who were neutral in the Civil War.

On 28 July 1922 at a meeting in Fermoy, Frank Daly and Professor O'Rahilly, put two specific questions to Liam Lynch: (1) Would he agree to cease hostilities if the other side did? and (2) in the event of the second Dáil meeting, would he recognise its authority?

The following day Lynch replied:

> ... when the Provisional Government cease their attack on us, defensive action on our part can cease ... If the Second Dáil, which is the Government of the Republic or any other elected assembly carry on such Government I see no difficulty as to allegiance of the army.[1]

Lynch's reply was sent to Michael Collins, together with two queries asking if he was prepared 'to arrange such a cessation of hostilities as General Liam Lynch intimates he is prepared to accept', and also if he would 'agree to call forthwith a meeting of the Second Dáil.'

Collins replied on 4 August:

> ... So far as the army is concerned I am merely obeying the orders of my Government and all the general staff and soldiers of the army merely carrying out the instructions given in accordance with such orders. This Government has made it fully clear that its desire is to secure obedience to proper authority. When an expression of such

obedience comes from the irregular leader I take it there will no longer be any necessity for arms conflict. When the irregulars – leaders and men – see fit to obey the wishes of the people, as expressed to their elected representatives, when they will give up their arms and cease their depredations on the persons and property of Irish citizens, there would be no longer need for hostility.[2]

Collins made it clear that this was an 'official answer as presumably your communication was meant to be addressed to the Government' and went on to refer to the form which prisoners, taken in the recent conflict, had been asked to sign and which most of them had refused. He therefore inferred from it that these men intended to take up arms again against the Provisional Government. 'If this is the spirit which animates Liam Lynch then I am sure your body will agree that it is very little good endeavouring to talk about terms.'[3] In this letter Collins referred to the duties of the government and to the fact that the time for face-saving had passed. 'The choice is definitely between the return of the British and the irregulars sending in their arms to the People's Government to be held in trust for the people.'[4] These were certainly strong words from a former friend and comrade.

On the same day, Arthur Griffith replying to two specific points, stated that the actions of the anti-treatyites were incorrectly described as being defensive and could therefore not be tolerated. He also stated that the functions of a second Dáil came to an end on 30 June 1922. In the letter Griffith insisted that the military action undertaken by the government was necessary to enforce obedience to parliament, which action would cease only when there was the surrender of arms, the restoration of seized property, and the restoration of bridges and roads which had been mined or made otherwise impassable.

The tone of these two letters indicate that the Provisional Government's intention to end the conflict was only through the absolute defeat and destruction of the anti-treaty forces. It should be noted that the Republican forces were, at this point, in a stronger position to negotiate than at any subsequent period. Though many favoured peace at almost any price, a large section of opinion disliked the fact that the Dáil had not continued to assemble, and they did not like the stand taken by the Provisional Government.

The situation, which Lynch envisaged, was an ideal one. He did not, however, take into account that the large majority of the people in Ireland wanted an end to the warfare. On 19 August 1922 he had directed, 'our troops will now be formed in ASU's [Active Service Units] and operate in the open'.[5] He stated that 'the strength of columns should not exceed thirty-five all ranks and that where a number of columns were operating in the same locality they should co-ordinate their security measures, afford each other mutual protection and act in combination when necessary.'[6]

During these months of the early part of the Civil War, Lynch had kept the progress of the conflict under review at frequent staff meetings: it could be said that the complete control of the Republican forces rested with him in so far as it was possible for any one man to exercise authority in the face of such a conflict. Lynch's optimistic nature was now strongly tinged with sadness. In a letter to his brother Tom on 16 September he wrote:

> The disaster of this war is sinking into my very bones, when I count the loss of Irish manhood and the general havoc of Civil War. Who could have dreamt that all our hopes could have been so blighted.

However, he had set out on a course and he was determined to see it through. He felt that nobody on the Republican side had any responsibility for carrying on the war except the Executive. De Valera expressed a desire to meet members of the army Executive, but Lynch was reluctant to hold an Executive meeting, unless 'the military situation improved considerably ... I would, however, be only too pleased to have your views, at any time on the general situation, and matters arising out of it, and they will receive my earnest consideration.'[7]

From the outset De Valera disagreed with the army split on

the treaty. Therefore, he was anxious that the members of the Executive would consider seriously the view that a military victory was not only impossible but virtually improbable. During the months from July to September, De Valera urged the leaders to try to end the conflict. This view was not now shared by Lynch. On his way to meet Liam Deasy in West Cork, De Valera called to Lynch at Fermoy. As soon as Dev left, Lynch sent a dispatch to Deasy: 'Dev's mission was to try to bring the war to an end. Give him no encouragement.'

On the evening of 22 August 1922, Michael Collins, commander-in-chief of the army, who had been on an inspection tour of military barracks in West Cork, was returning to the city when he was shot dead at Beal-na-mBláth. Republican officers had gathered in the area for a meeting to determine future strategy. Collins was in a military convoy that passed through the locality that morning. He was recognised. As this was an enemy convoy passing through Republican held territory, they decided to set up an ambush. The following day Liam Deasy sent a dispatch to Liam Lynch giving just an outline account of what happened. Lynch acknowledged Deasy's correspondence as follows:

Irish Republic Army,
Field General Headquarters,
Department C/S,
C/O 1st Southern Division   22 August 1922

A Chara,
1. Yours of the 24th inst. reporting attack on the enemy at Beal-na-mBláth to hand yesterday.
2. Considering the very small number of men engaged this was a most successful operation, and they are to be complimented on the fight made under such heavy fire, and against such odds.
3. Considering you were aware of the fact that the convoy contained an armoured car, it is surprising you had not mines laid to get this.
4. Nothing could bring home more forcibly the awful unfortunate national situation at present than the fact that it has become necessary for Irishmen and former comrades to shoot such men as M. Collins who rendered such splendid service to the Republic in the late war against England. It is to be hoped our present

enemies will realise the folly in trying to crush the Republic before it is too late.

Mise le Meas
Liam Lynch C/S.[8]

It was Paddy O'Brien's belief that, 'when Collins, the one man on the other side prepared to negotiate, was gone, Liam became more determined. He knew the others were not prepared to compromise, therefore it became a fight to the finish.'[9]

Liam Deasy was convinced that the tragedy of the Civil War was that the anti-treatyites' protests did not end with the fall of the Four Courts. (It is, of course, easy to accept this view with hindsight, but the inter-action of that time did not lend itself to such an idealistic situation.) Deasy was, at this juncture in August, pulled between De Valera's call for peace, and Lynch's 'faith that somehow the Staters would have to surrender.'[10]

On 30 August Very Rev. Monsignor O'Hagan, Rector of the Irish College in Rome who was in Ireland, wrote to Richard Mulcahy requesting a meeting between Liam Mellows, Rory O'Connor, Oscar Traynor and Tom Barry, then in jail. Richard Mulcahy agreed to the meeting in Mountjoy Jail. O'Connor and Mellows, having received a copy of the letter, jointly wrote stating that they welcomed 'any efforts promising to end this new and unnatural attack on the independence of the country'. Copies of both letters were sent to Lynch who was still in the south.

Monsignor O'Hagan met Ernie O'Malley in Dublin and some proposals were put forward. Lynch's comment was 'that they were not worth much consideration by us'.

In the period following Collins' death Emmet Dalton in Cork worked in association with Tom Ennis to find a peace formula.[11] Deasy told Liam Lynch about this, stating 'that intermediaries were trying to make contact.' Lynch's response was 'that these men were undoubtedly acting on Government orders, and he asked why didn't they contact him directly.'

'Is anyone foolish enough to believe that either of them [Ennis or Dalton] would negotiate without orders of Government? Then why not direct negotiations?'[12]

Is this the key that would have opened the door to peace? Did Lynch feel slighted because he was not approached directly? After all, a meeting was arranged and held near Crookstown on 13 October between Tom Ennis and Charlie Russell on the Provisional Government side and Liam Deasy and Tom Barry on the Republican side. (Dalton had dropped out of the negotiations.)

It was confirmed that General Dalton was acting on definite instructions from the minister for defence (Mulcahy) and was anxious 'to make an effort towards ending the present needless strife on the basis of an unconditional surrender'.[13] It was Ernest Bythe's belief that 'Lynch was totally uncompromising. He was determined to fight it to the end; but so were we.'[14]

Prior to the Civil War, Todd Andrews found Liam Mellows rather critical of 'Liam Lynch for placing too much trust in Collins and Mulcahy's good intentions. Frank Aiken pleaded with both Mulcahy and Lynch to resist from hostilities, as he himself was determined that there was not going to be a Civil War – at least not in his division …'

Andrews was aware that 'from as early as August, De Valera was convinced of the impossibility of winning the war and wanted to call it off, but Liam Lynch made it clear to him that any public action to this end would be repudiated by the Executive and the fighting would continue.' Emmet Dalton wanted the Civil War to end, especially following Collins' death. 'I was really sick of it all when as the months progressed and I saw the turn events were taking.'

But why didn't he make contact with Liam Lynch? 'My efforts even with Tom Barry and Deasy did not get very far,' responded Dalton. Wasn't Dalton's demand 'an unconditional surrender'? 'This was, after all, the superior military stage which we had reached. The discussions with Liam Lynch could follow if there was some platform of agreement.'[15]

By September 1922 De Valera was extremely anxious to bring both sides together and to pursue his aim through political means.

According to Mulcahy, De Valera explained to him that he [De Valera] was not responsible for what the leaders of his side believed, nor was he able to get them to understand his point of view. He was endeavouring to find a basis for peace and wondered if there was any method in which the treaty decisions could be revised. But Mulcahy, who met Dev, informed him that the treaty was not negotiable. By this time, it was quite clear that the control of the anti-treatyites was totally outside De Valera's influence, and as time progressed Liam Lynch was the man in command, so De Valera was compelled to do as Lynch suggested.

Rev. Fr Wall, Broadford, wrote to Lynch on 13 October pointing out that Mulcahy's response to Monsignor O'Hagan was that he and his army were carrying on 'a defensive war' which would cease if the anti-treatyites ceased firing on his men. Lynch took a cold look at Mulcahy's 'defensive attitude' which he stated 'is only quibbling with the situation. What a defensive action to first attack our GHQ and other positions all over the country! When he ceases to attack us in our efforts to maintain the Republic, then there will be peace.'

He continued by insisting on more definite proposals. 'The fight must go on until there is no question of forcing Ireland into the British Empire, by the enemy, foreign or domestic.'[16]

Towards the end of September 1922 casualties had mounted to over 300 killed or wounded and there were over 6,000 Republican prisoners either in jails or internment camps. The arms' position was by this time reasonably satisfactory and guerrilla warfare seemed to be working fairly well.

The Provisional Government issued a proclamation giving effect to a decision to set up military courts with powers to inflict the death penalty; the decision had been carried by eighty votes to eighteen in the Provisional parliament on 27 September.[17] A Free State document, 7 October 1922 stated:

> If prisoners are taken they must not be released until they are incapable of further harm. If executions are necessary they must be

carried out with no fear of the chimera of popular reaction.

The Irish hierarchy met on the same day at Maynooth and stated that armed resistance was 'morally only a system of murder and assassination of the national forces'.

The Provisional Government casualties up to the middle of September were 185 killed and 674 wounded. A tragic feature of the entire operation was that men who had fought bravely together against the British, now died on opposite sides of the camp – men like Cathal Brugha, Harry Boland, Michael Collins and Arthur Griffith (who died in Dublin on 12 August, due to exhaustion). Republican prisoners were now in over-crowded jails and internment camps. Lynch had forbidden hunger strikes where political treatment was granted. On the Republican side, all prisoners taken were released unharmed once their arms and ammunition were taken from them, mainly because they did not have accommodation for them. It was an absurd situation.

Éamon de Valera wanted a public declaration by the army Executive of the actual existing situation. 'The Army Executive must publicly accept responsibility ... There must be no doubt in the minds of anybody in this matter. This pretence from the pro-treaty party that we are inciting the army must be ended by the declaration from the army itself that this is not so.'[18] It was therefore necessary to call the Executive together though doing so involved risk. Liam Lynch issued instructions to have the meeting called.

When the men on the army Executive met in Nugents, Bally-bacon on 16 October 1922, Liam Lynch presided. It was decided to co-opt four members to replace those imprisoned, substitutes were named and ratified by the entire body. A day of negotiations was devoted to a review of events since the outbreak of hostilities and to the consideration of certain peace proposals. Lynch stated that it was decided, at the Clarence Hotel meeting after the attack on the Four Courts, that each division would operate on its own and that there would be no headquarters outside the Four Courts. However, he must have become convinced soon afterwards that this would not give the best results as he subsequently created three commands, Northern and Eastern to be commanded by Ernie O'Malley, Western under the control of Michael Kilroy and Southern commanded by Liam Deasy.

The meeting continued the following day (17 October) with eleven members of the army Executive present. Two important points were discussed:

> First – whether the forces should continue to wage war under the authority of the Executive only or whether the Executive itself should sanction and co-operate in the formation of a Republican government – this would control the Republican forces and continue in armed resistance against the Provisional Government. Second – a policy decision on what minimum terms of peace would be acceptable.[19]

De Valera had sent Liam Lynch a memorandum which Lynch read to the meeting. This memorandum suggested that if a decision was taken to continue the fight, then the possibility of setting up a Republican government which would co-ordinate efforts and prevent a Free State government from establishing itself, should be considered; it would also mean laying claims to any funds or resources of the Republic. He stated that the only public policy necessary was to maintain the Republic and the sovereign independence of the nation: also he suggested that there should be a frank exchange of views and a definite understanding between the army and the government.[20] Following lengthy discussions at this meeting, the members of the Executive realising that the problem was not solely a military one, expressed an almost unanimous feeling in favour of the establishment of a Republican government. A resolution was passed which called on 'the former president of Dáil Éireann to form a Government which will preserve the continuity of the Republic'. The Executive pledged wholehearted support provided 'arrangement does not bring the country into the British Empire. Final decision on this question to be submitted for ratification to the Executive'.

On 25 October the available Republican deputies met secretly in Dublin, constituted themselves as the Republican government, and appointed De Valera as president with a twelve-member council of state. A proclamation was issued by the army Executive on 28 October and it was arranged that documents from the defence department would be signed both by De Valera, as president, and Liam Lynch, chief-of-staff. While De Valera recognised the views of Lynch and the Executive he made his position clear in a letter to Joe McGarrity: 'If the Army thinks I am too moderate, well, let them try to get a better President and go ahead.'[21]

An army council had also been appointed at the Executive meeting. This consisted of Liam Lynch, Ernie O'Malley, Liam Deasy, Tom Derrig and Frank Aiken. Three members were also appointed to replace any member of the council who was killed or captured (Joe O'Connor, Con Moloney, Michael Kilroy). Following a meeting of the Republican Army Executive, Lynch expressed his satisfaction in a letter to his brother, Tom:

> It was a splendid review of the actual situation all over Ireland ... We are absolutely confident that the Free State is beaten and that it is only a matter of time when they must give in. Recently, we have been offered very broad terms, to their mind; but when they still stand in the way of independence we cannot accept them. We will accept no terms which brings Ireland into the British Empire.[22]

Lynch now decided to move his headquarters to Dublin, as this would be advantageous from a communications point of view. Since he had come south at the end of June, he had maintained communication with Dublin through the valuable efforts of Kathleen Barry, a courier. Following the evacuation of Fermoy barracks in August, he remained in the First and Second Southern Division area, and stayed in houses in his old brigade area. On 20 September Kathleen Barry met him at Killavullen to accompany him to Rossadrehid in the Glen of Aherlow. He broke the journey to make a brief call home. While he was in the Glen, his brother, Tom, now a priest, cycled from Anglesboro to see him On 14 October, accompanied by Con Moloney, Moss Twomey and Matt Ryan, Liam left the Glen to cross the Galtees to Ballybacon for the Executive meeting. Having stayed at McGrath's for a night, he travelled, mostly on foot, through south Kilkenny, Wexford, Carlow and Wicklow to Dublin where he arrived on 3 November 1922.

The Dublin headquarters was established at Tower House, Santry. This large house had a secret room which was specially constructed. The secret room was used to conceal men at the frequently held meetings, also weapons, documents, typewriter and other evidence of the presence of so many people. Here Liam and his staff were the guests of the Cassidy and Fitzgerald families. Both families were extremely kind, helpful and thorough in their cover-up; indeed while Liam was there, no attention was drawn to him or his comrades' presence or to their headquarters.[23]

Just two days after Lynch's arrival in Dublin, Ernie O'Malley was captured having been seriously wounded in a fight. On 17 November the first executions under the Provisional Government legislation took place (four young men who were armed when captured). Erskine Childers was shot on 24 November and on the same day Michael Kilroy, O/C Western Command was wounded and captured. Frank Barrett O/C First Western Division reported at the end of the month that 'as a result of the capture by the enemy of nearly all the best officers in the area the organisation showed very grave signs of collapse, consequently all our energies are directed towards re-organising.'

It was with shock that Lynch watched the new twist which the Civil War was taking; the Provisional Government's policy of executions grieved him as did the atrocities carried out by the pro-treaty forces. In a letter to the Provisional Government, dated 27 November (a copy of which he sent to Thomas Johnson, chairman of the parliamentary Labour Party), he protested that they had 'declared war on the soldiers of the Republic and suppressed the legitimate parliament of the Irish nation':

As your Parliament and Army Headquarters well know, we on our side have at all times adhered to the recognised rules of warfare. In the early days of this war we took hundreds of your forces prisoners but accorded them all the rights of prisoners of war and, over and above, treated them as fellow countrymen and former comrades. Many of your soldiers have been released by us three times although captured with arms on each occasion. But the prisoners you have taken have been treated barbarously, and when helpless you have tortured, wounded and murdered them ...

Next to the members of your 'Provisional Government' every member of your body who voted for this resolution by which you pretend to make legal the murder of soldiers, is equally guilty. We therefore give you and each member of your body due notice that unless your army recognises the rules of warfare in future we shall adopt very drastic measures to protect our forces.[24]

On 30 November, he issued an order, which was captured, stating that 'all members of the Provisional "Parliament" who were present and voted for the Murder Bill will be shot at sight.'[25] Following this on 7 December, Dáil deputy Seán Hales was shot dead, though being absent he had not voted. Controversy has surrounded this shooting, as Deputy Pádraig Ó Maille, who was travelling with him, was also shot but not seriously wounded.

Early next morning four men who had been prisoners since the fall of the Four Courts at the end of June (Rory O'Connor, Liam Mellows, Joe McKelvey and Dick Barrett) were taken from their cells in Mountjoy and executed.

The Free State had officially come into existence on 6 December 1922, and now the Civil War had taken on a cruel and bitter twist.

Meanwhile, down south Tom Barry, who had escaped from Gormanstown in September, had been planning a major blow against the Provisional Government forces. Shortly after his escape, Lynch had appointed him operations officer, Southern Command. Later Lynch appointed him director of operations, in charge of all divisional O/Cs. By early November, aided by several districts officers in the Southern Division Barry had organised a massive 580 riflemen: they encircled Cork city, held all roads to Macroom, Bandon, Kinsale, Cobh. In this daring operation Barry's strategic plan secured many Cork towns for the Republicans. He mobilised men to take Bandon, then the twin towns of Ballineen and Enniskeane, then Ballinvourney, Ballingeary and many other towns and villages in west and mid Cork.

With Lynch, Barry organised a selection of men to prepare for a northern offensive. Lynch was convinced that Barry's military genius would pull the war in the Republicans' favour. Barry secured men from the Southern Division, as well as guns and ammunition to travel to Donegal for the first leg of the journey to attack Derry. Barry hoped this would bring the Provisional Government into a decision to join in a united attack against Britain. His belief was that as a united army they could fight the common cause of Ireland.

With a few selected experienced column leaders from the Cork brigades and a force from the Second Southern Division, he went to Tipperary and with Dinny Lacy and a group of Tipperary men he organised a combined attack on Free State posts at Callan, Mullinavat, Thomastown and Carrick-on-Suir during the early days of December. According to Dan Cahalane, 'he marched through villages and towns where they hardly stood to fight. They practically handed the places over to him.' His reputation as a daring elusive commander, the man who could neither be held nor killed, had made him into a legendary figure. He had plans to develop the offensive northwards by an attack on Templemore where he hoped to capture artillery, thus enabling him to attack the Curragh and then on to the capital, Dublin. The winter and the war dragged on and Barry's plans were frustrated by the rapid change in the situation in the early months of 1923.

During the closing days of 1922 and the early days of 1923 the outlook for the Republican forces was not hopeful, yet men were facing it with great fortitude. The executions of prisoners in jails and the deaths of leaders on both sides added to the horror of the situation. Lynch was well aware that his own life was in danger and that at any time death was close. He wrote a letter from Tower House to his mother on 22 December:

> I do pray that many weeks of the New Year shall not pass before the Civil War ends, but really I have not much hope of an early ending as our present enemy still insists on dishonouring the nation by forcing her into the British Empire. If I should happen to be murdered by fellow Irishmen I'll die with an intense love for the national Irish people, and on behalf of my comrades of the IRA who have stood up to the British Empire for years, sincerely forgive the Irish people who unintentionally wish to dishonour the nation ... Would that England's hounds had tracked me down rather than old comrades who have been false to their allegiance. Future generations can best judge our actions, and these will be proud we so acted at a vital period. After the present, propaganda, materialism and war-weariness hide the brave sacrifices that are being made by our forces.[26]

Con Moloney, who understood exactly what was happening in the south, wrote to Lynch from the Glen of Aherlow on 4 December 1922 and told him not to think military victory would be possible as they faced a stone wall, also that local initiative was dead, and discipline had relaxed. Lynch in his reply agreed that the position in the west was far from satisfactory but added that he was determined to continued to fight: 'The loss of leaders and sacrifices from week to week cannot under any circumstances bring us to lessen our demands.' The following day Lynch issued a circular on peace moves in which he stated 'no terms short of Independence can be accepted by Army or Government.'

Day and night he worked, endeavouring to foster an atmosphere of confidence and optimism in the other officers. He was convinced that the Republican forces could maintain almost indefinitely the kind of opposition to the Provisional Government forces which would eventually cause them to accede. He believed he could create a situation which would force the treatyites to abandon their cause, surrender to the old movement, and in a united effort demand a less humiliating settlement with Britain.

By this stage he had lost faith in the sincerity of Free State proposals, believing that their general policy was to split the solidarity of the army Executive. Not even De Valera's request earlier in August could wean his mind from the course in which it had now been set. De Valera also wrote to Lynch suggesting that it was their duty to meet the Free State in some form of political basis. 'It has always been my view that with anything like goodwill on both sides a constitutional way out of this impasse could be found.'[27] But even though military victory was out of reach, Lynch's outlook remained unchanged.

Liam Deasy

Determination and hope of victory

Though Liam Lynch saw what was happening in Ireland, he was, nevertheless, aware of the intervention of Britain in affairs since the outbreak of the Civil War. On 30 January 1923 he made a detailed report to the president and ministers stating that:

> When the Civil War broke out orders were issued from the Four Courts to wage war on England but owing to disorganisation nothing could be done. At the last meeting of the Executive the matter was again discussed, but though action was very much favoured I was not in a position to recommend it, as we had not a staff in charge and no satisfactory organisation.

He now believed that his forces in England were sufficiently well organised and equipped to undertake operations in specific areas, and suggested that hostilities against the common enemy should be undertaken. Whether or not this suggestion was a ploy for unity, the rapid changes in the situation in Ireland certainly cancelled out any plans which he may have had for an offensive in Britain.

By the end of January 1923 guerrilla warfare was almost over. Fighting was reduced to sniping attacks between opposing forces. Fifty-five executions had been carried out and many more were pending. The Free State authorities had introduced a policy of sentencing prisoners to death in places where Republican activities were taking place, consequently the conflict now lacked any human dignity. It seemed that the Free State forces were out to win the struggle no matter how ruthless the methods. It was evident that military victory was no longer a possibility, yet doggedly and stubbornly both sides continued the battle.

The Republicans seemed prepared to continue fighting even though their strength had been steadily whittled down, with lives being lost daily; their actions were outlawed by the church; the majority of the people and the morale of their forces was weakening. Tom Barry, Liam Deasy and men at ground level began to see that victory was impossible and that negotiations should be undertaken. Liam Deasy was captured on 18 January as he lay sick in a house in Tincurry. Previous to this he had been formulating proposals to end the conflict as he realised that further resistance was useless. He was aware of the responsibility which he held, but unfortunately his arrest did not help the situation. No longer free and trapped into making a decision, he felt obliged to avail of the only means his captors left open to him; faced with death, he decided that there was no point in continuing, as many more of his comrades would be executed by the Free State government,[1] therefore he signed a document dictated to him which agreed to an unconditional surrender of all arms and men as required by General Mulcahy:

> ... in pursuance of this undertaking I am asked to appeal for a similar undertaking and acceptance from the following: E. de Valera, P. Ruttledge, A. Stack, M. Colivet, Domhnal O'Callaghan, Liam Lynch, Con Moloney, T. Derrig, F. Aiken, S. Barrett, T. Barry, S. McSwiney, Séamus Robinson, Humphrey Murphy, Séamus O'Donovan, Frank Carthy and for the immediate and unconditional surrender of themselves after the issue by them of an order for surrender on the part of all those associated with them, together with their arms and equipment.[2]

Though not looked on at the time as a courageous stand Liam Deasy's appeal was subsequently regarded as such. Copies of it, together with a long covering letter in which Deasy set out the reasons which impelled him to make it, were delivered to the members of the government and army Executive by Fr Tom Duggan who had been nominated as courier by Liam Deasy. The Free State government did not publish the document immediately but waited until 9 February 1923 and gave it the widest publicity in conjunction with a similar appeal made by prisoners in Limerick.

The policy of executions initially begun in November 1922 continued to mount with ruthless vigour.[3] On 20 January 1923 eleven prisoners were shot, two in Limerick, four in Tralee, five in Athlone. On 22 January three men were executed in Dundalk, on 23 January two in Waterford, on 26 January two more were shot in Birr and on the next day two were executed in Maryboro. Not even the terrible cost in blood, in sorrow and in sadness, not even the bleak prospect that failure may be nigh, not even the appeals of former, now neutral, comrades nor of church leaders or of friends could alter Lynch's determination to continue the struggle in arms. He stood firmly in the role in which he had set out, and replied:

> I am to inform you officially, on behalf of the Government and Army Command, that the proposal contained in your circular letter of 30 January, and the enclosure, cannot be considered.

Comrades say that because he lived in Dublin during this period, his appreciation of the true situation was far more optimistic than the facts warranted. Maurice Twomey, general headquarters staff, gives a picture of Liam at that time:

> He could not or would not face the thought of defeat and collapse of Republican resistance to the imposition of the Treaty. The farthest he would allow himself to think in such a direction was that the Free State authorities would be compelled to negotiate with Republicans. Abandonment of the struggle in the field he would not countenance, and I believe this would have continued to be his attitude if he had not been killed. I feel that in no circumstances would he himself surrender, and that he would never order those under his command to do so.[4]

Ernie O'Malley, who was in jail at this time, got a letter out to Liam Lynch with his criticism of Deasy's activity. 'Prisoners are casualties and must not be considered ...' He further expressed his opinion that the public would swing to which ever side they felt would win. 'The chaplain came to me with a paper yesterday and hinted that I should follow Deasy's example and also that of the Limerick prisoners; I'm glad I managed to contain myself when he was in my cell, but when he left I went up in smoke.'[5]

The following day O'Malley got another letter out to Lynch which indicated that the deputy governor had been attempting to persuade the Mountjoy men to sign the unconditional surrender; but he advised Lynch to have courage as the '... enemy government will realise that even if the leaders go, the rank and file will carry on ...'⁶ This type of encouragement gave Lynch renewed vigour.

De Valera, in a letter to McGarrity, regarded Deasy's surrender statement as 'the biggest blow we have got since we started'.⁷ Liam Lynch told McGarrity that Deasy was 'in a despondent mood' and his attitude was that 'there can be no going back on our demands. It is clear the enemy will carry out many executions, but even though this terrible sacrifice has to take place we must put up with the consequences.'⁸

It was Lynch's intention towards the last day of January to visit the south 'in a few weeks';⁹ however the many activities which crowded his days meant he had to postpone the visit. He made an appeal to his forces to make an all-out effort to compel the Free State authorities into the position of negotiation.

From the outset of the Civil War he endeavoured to conduct the conflict on recognised warfare lines, and in an 'Order' dated 27 September 1922 he had prohibited retaliation despite the fact that 'some cruel and cold blooded murders' had been committed against 'our troops' but 'similar reprisals for these murders cannot under any circumstances be tolerated.'¹⁰

In the same order he prohibited the shooting of unarmed Free State soldiers and the use of explosive ammunition; wounded enemy personnel should receive proper medical attention; the hoisting of the white flag denoting surrender should be accepted. In the Mulcahy papers there are copies of alleged 'captured documents' one issued to 'O/Cs all battalions' dated 23 November 1922 and a further document which is entitled 'Enemy Murder Bill' and dated 30 November 1922 in which it is stated that, 'All members of the Provisional "Parliament" who, were present and voted for the Murder Bill will be shot at sight ... Houses of members of Murder Bill, active supporters of P.G. who are known to support Murder Bill will be destroyed ... Free State army officers who approve of Murder Bill will be shot at sight; also all ex-British army officers and men who joined the Free State army since

170

6 December 1921.'[11] The order was 'to be duplicated and transmitted to O/C all units.' This alleged document came to light when an inquest was being held on the death of Hugh Houghton, Dublin. According to the *Irish Independent* 15 March 1923 report, 'a Colonel in the national army identified the signature on a captured document produced as that of Liam Lynch, chief-of-staff in the Irregular army.'[12] But without investigation could it be identified categorically and stated with certainty that a signature was that of a particular person?

In a 'Proclamation' of 1 February, Lynch as chief-of-staff expressed his revulsion at the unethical practices of the Free State government 'who have resorted to the infamous practice of shooting Republican soldiers taken by them as prisoners of war, and have already put to death fifty-three officers and men in this manner, "and having violated with impunity" the "international usages of war" this "Junta" have announced "that Punitive Action" will be taken against other prisoners in their power if hostages which we have been compelled to take are not set at liberty. *Now We Hereby Give Notice* that we shall not give up our hostages, and if threatened action be taken, we shall hold every member of the said Junta and its so-called Parliament, Senate and other House, and all their Executives responsible, and shall certainly visit them with the punishment they shall deserve'.[13]

A further 'Captured Document' order issued to 'O/C battalion III' states:

> The following will be shot at sight ... (a) all members who voted for Enemy Murder Bill; (b) officials of all rank; (c) members of senate in list A; (d) members of Murder Gang; (e) officials – civilians who order prisoners to be fired on; (f) those who torture prisoners ...

The order goes on to list a number of targets such as 'high court, county and district judges and state solicitors ... editors and leader-writers of hostile press in Ireland in cases where these are known to be hostile ...' It also lists the residences belonging to certain owners which 'shall be destroyed.[14]

The documents published in the *Freeman's Journal* 16 March

1923 are similar but not identical to those found in the Mulcahy papers – those published in the newspaper appeal on the surface at least to go beyond Lynch's dictum of having 'honourably stood by the rules of War', because the alleged 'Captured Documents' in the newspaper states that 'aggressive civilian supporters of the Free State government policy of executions of prisoners of war [and] ... officials (civilian or military) employed at the headquarters of the different enemy Ministries', as 'enemies of the Republic will be shot at sight ...'[15]

On 4 December 1922, which was four days after the alleged captured documents were issued, a document under the heading 'General Activities' was signed by Liam Lynch, which is among the alleged 'Captured Documents' in the Mulcahy Papers. In this, document he again talks about the rules of war:

> ... We have met the enemy in noble warfare, putting our weak arm against his strong one ... We have not adopted against him the same tactics adopted against the British ... While our prisoners have been murdered and tortured ... all efforts will be concentrated on making the enemy realise that no matter what the cost may be, no government but that of the Republic will ever function in Ireland. The maintenance of discipline is the first duty of officers and they will take special care to see that no matter what tactics the enemy descends to, the honour of the IRA will be preserved inviolate.[16]

According to Florence O'Donoghue, 'even in the face of persistent Free State policy of executing prisoners of war, he [Lynch] continued steadily to resist any departure from the letter or spirit of the order, beyond the taking and holding of hostages.'[17] On 1 February 1923, Lynch issued a strongly-worded proclamation denouncing the 'Government of the Irish Free State'.[18]

Lynch was keenly aware of adverse propaganda. The *War News* issued by the Free State government carried stories, which were often exaggerated, and these were often reprinted in the daily newspapers.[19]

On 10 February, he sent a formal letter of protest to Richard Mulcahy setting out in detail the breaches of 'civilised warfare' ethics such as the 'shooting of prisoners' without trial; prisoners taken from lorries and murdered by the roadside; the wounded deprived of proper medical attention. In this document he outlined full details of the breaches with names and dates. He was convinced that military resistance to the treaty should continue as long as the treaty included partition and enforced inclusion in the British empire.

In a letter to Con Moloney he stated that 'were it not for recent events we would have forced them to accept our terms within a few weeks'.[20] It seems likely that he was referring to Liam Deasy's order of unconditional surrender. Lynch remained adamant and would not entertain any suggestion of seeking terms, because according to Liam Deasy:

> Being an idealist, his highest principles were his guide. It was not in his nature to surrender or to compromise. It is my opinion that the promise he made to support the Four Courts garrison, if they were attacked remained a sacred trust, and the two broken treaties which he had signed in Limerick with Donnacha O'Hannigan and Michael Brennan confirmed his determination that this would be a fight to the finish.

Deasy maintained that De Valera had no illusions and had stated that a military victory was not possible. 'Once De Valera saw that Lynch and his men had to burn Fermoy barracks and abandon the vast territory he told me that he could not see any hope of a military victory.'

Deasy also maintained that Seán Hyde was extremely enthusiastic about the position of the anti-treaty forces and could not understand the meaning of the word defeat and it was his belief that Hyde's enthusiastic reports to Liam Lynch 'did much to encourage and strengthen Liam in his determination to carry on the fight. This, despite the fact, that the edifice seemed to be crumbling around us.' (Hyde was in the south – Lynch was in Dublin at that time.) [21]

Lynch resisted all demands for a meeting of the Executive. In a letter of 22 January to the members of the Army Council he stated: 'It was impossible for the Executives to meet' as he was convinced it would be dangerous if they were all together in one place. In this letter he asked that the council would continue to report on any developments, and freely express their views.

Tom Barry and Tom Crofts went to Dublin and on 6 February requested that an Executive meeting should be called and they stressed the importance of Lynch's attendance. P. J. Ruttledge was also convinced of the need for an Executive meeting. He wrote to De Valera saying, 'It is absolutely essential that the Army Executive meet to review the situation and decide, when conversant with all circumstances and conditions, as to the prosecution of the war or otherwise.'[22] Barry and Crofts returned to the First Southern Division headquarters near Ballyvourney on 9 February 1923, and held a division council meeting at Cronin's in Gougane Barra on 10 February. The following day they drafted a letter to Lynch and repeated their request for a meeting of the Executive. In this they were supported by Humphrey Murphy and Seán McSwiney. Lynch had intended leaving Dublin for the south on 9 February, but replying to correspondence delayed him until the thirteenth.

In the early days of 1923 Lynch sent for Todd Andrews. 'I'm going to pull the south together,' he said, and suggested taking Andrews with him as his adjutant. Following some questions by Lynch, Andrews told him that the situation throughout the country was anything but hopeful. However, Lynch discounted his pessimism and was cheered by Andrew's account of conditions in south Wexford which in general were rather hopeful. Though Lynch was disappointed at Deasy's surrender appeal he told Andrews that he felt sure he could restore the situation from a base in the south. 'I pointed out, rather timidly, that we didn't seem to have any coherent plan of action either at local, brigade or divisional level.' Todd Andrews said that in February, De Valera brought back Document No. 2 and this angered Lynch who responded:

Your publicity as to sponsoring Document No. 2 has had a very bad effect on the army and should have been avoided. Generally they do not understand such documents. We can arrange a peace without referring to past documents.[23]

De Valera responded in a long letter making no apologies for his opinions: 'Many good men have come to the conclusion that we have long ago passed the point at which we should have regarded ourselves as beaten so far as actually securing our objective is concerned ...'[24] Lynch was now going to meet the men 'on the ground' and was confident he would prove De Valera wrong.

Before leaving Dublin Liam said goodbye to Madge Clifford. It was as if he might have had a premonition of his death. His parting words were, 'You may never see me again!' He had a great family grievance to bear. His brother, Jack (Seán) had been arrested and was in Maryboro jail, listed with so many others, for execution.

Commandant Paddy Brennan, O/C South Dublin brigade, arranged transport and protection for Dr Con Lucy and Lynch to Templeogue and on to Ballymore Eustace and then to Borris where they were joined by Todd Andrews and John Dowling. Travelling mainly at night, very often with the car lights switched off, they occasionally changed to a pony and trap and continued on their journey southwards. It was a slow, tedious nerve-wrecking journey to Kilkenny where they met Martin McGrath, then on to Foskins in Mooncoin where they stayed for a few days.

During this journey Andrews got to know Lynch well and at night-time the two discussed the country's position. According to Andrews, Lynch often spoke of his former comrades and it was with 'a countenance more in sorrow than in anger'. He found it inexplicable, Andrews said, how Collins, of all people, could have started the Civil War which would bring the nation 'under the sovereignty of the British Crown or how he could have accepted partition'. Requests had often been put to Lynch to allow Free State soldiers armed or unarmed to be shot as reprisals for the executions which the Free State government was continuing to pursue, but this was something Lynch refused to countenance. 'Liam thought that shooting prisoners was immoral; he wondered how as Christians the Free Staters justified such to their own consciences.' According to Andrews, 'Lynch was a simple, uncomplicated man, believing deeply in God, the Blessed Virgin and the Saints, and in loving Ireland as he did he had dedicated his life to her under God.' Throughout it all he felt no bitterness towards his opponents in the Provisional Government, nor the Free State army, only sadness that they had dishonoured Ireland. 'To the end he believed that had Collins taken the lead events would have followed a different course.'[25]

Dan Breen in jail in 1923
(Courtesy, Cork Public Museum)

Seán Fitzpartick, Dan Breen and Con Moloney in Tipperary 1923
(Courtesy, Cork Public Museum)

With Executive members

It was cold and continuously wet during the ten days of their journey south. Lynch, Con Lucy and Andrews had been travelling mainly by night. In a pony and trap they forded the Tar River and were lucky to escape drowning as the pony stumbled several times. While in Araglin (22 February) they met David Kent, brother of the Kent boys who had resisted the British in 1916. (This incident had given Liam Lynch his first inspiration to join the volunteers.)

The men now had to travel mainly on foot and because Lynch had been confined so long at Tower House, Dublin, his physical fitness had deteriorated somewhat so he rested at Araglin, his old brigade area for only a short period. On receipt of a dispatch from West Cork stating that there was a move towards peace, Lynch could wait no longer. Determined to put an end to the peace talks, he gave Todd Andrews a dispatch telling him to go to Con Moloney and inform him of his (Lynch's) decision – that he wished to add new life to his forces.

Andrews cautiously crossed the Galtee Mountains to discover that Con Moloney had been arrested, but he met Dan Breen who informed him that the situation in the south appeared to be deteriorating. Andrews felt it was imperative to get back immediately with the news to Lynch.

Following a meeting of Cork No. 2 brigade council, Lynch had resumed his hazardous journey to the First Southern Division headquarters near Ballyvourney. With Con Lucy, Lynch crossed the Blackwater at Killavullen and continued through Donoghmore and on towards Lehanes of Ballingeary where they arrived on 26 February 1923. The First Southern Division council meeting was reconvened at James Moynihans, in Coolea, on 26 February and lasted for almost three days – eighteen officers attended, and only three were absent. Four members who were present – Tom Barry, Tom Crofts, Humphrey Murphy and Seán McSwiney demanded that a meeting of the army Executive be held which had been endorsed by the general council (at its meeting on the tenth.) The proposal was put forward again at this meeting and Lynch said that he 'alone was responsible for not calling it.' He felt that there was no point in calling a meeting as the present Executive had no power to make peace or war because the imprisoned members would have to be released in order to produce a comprehensive decision. 'If he thought he could not carry on successfully he would not allow the war to continue for a moment longer and would put the matter to the [Republican] government.'[1]

Each of the eighteen officers of the Southern Division at this three-day council meeting openly expressed their opinion on the military situation. The division O/C reported:

> ... We are fought to a standstill, and at present we are flattened out ... The men are suffering great privations, and their morale is going ... These men have been continually going for years back ... quite satisfied to carry on until Executive meeting when he [O/C] will satisfy himself on the following points: (1) What are we fighting for? (2) Can we win militarily?... The majority, while believing that military victory was no longer a possibility expressed a willingness to continue the struggle though, 'the present forces against us will cripple us eventually, and we cannot hope to last against them'.[2]

They emphasised that because of reduced strength, diminished ammunition supplies and the difficulty of their position they would have to operate on a smaller scale with fewer units.

Lynch, listening to the men who had the pulse of the situation, was receiving a much more realistic view of the position than he could have visualised from headquarters in Dublin. He was aware, he told the meeting, that the southern counties were opposed by the heaviest concentration of Free State troops in the country; it was his view also that the peace offensive would be made mainly against the south. The relative strength of their forces was discussed, and Tom Barry emphasised strongly that in the entire country their strength did not exceed 8,000.[3] This number was opposed by the Free State authorities with a build up force of at least 38,000 combat troops, with the extra facilities of barracks, armoured cars and artillery. Lynch felt that a meeting of the Executive could be risky. But, as he listened to the outspoken opinion of men whom he knew well for their loyalty and fighting quality, he became more convinced that they were in a crisis situation, therefore it was imperative that an Executive meeting should be held.

When the conference ended he wrote to Con Moloney expressing his resentment of action taken on the part of some officers who were inclined to work independently of GHQ. 'What they mean by acting on their own views I cannot understand. However, I hope we are now done with it.'

It emerged from this meeting that Lynch was determined the fight should go on, despite the fact that some of the members of the First Southern Division were beginning to lose confidence. He was convinced that eventually the Free State government would be forced to enter into some form of negotiations as emphasised in a long letter, which he wrote to Con Moloney, dated 29 March: 'I still have an optimistic view of the situation; if we can hold the army fast all will be well.'[4] However, instead things began to take a turn for the worse.

A tragic sequence of death and captures were to follow. Denny Lacey, O/C Tipperary, had been killed on 18 February 1923 in the Glen of Aherlow. Con Moloney was wounded and captured after a fight in the Glen. His brother Jim, intelligence officer of the Southern Command and Tom Conway O/C communications, who were wounded in that fight, were also taken prisoners. (Tom Derrig replaced Con Moloney as adjutant general and Lynch himself temporarily took over the duties of the command O/C.) In Knocknagoshal, Co. Kerry when three Free State officers and two men were killed in a mine trap, nine Republican prisoners were taken from Tralee jail as a reprisal, they were tied together and placed over a mine at Ballyseedy on 7 March. When the mine was exploded, eight of the prisoners were shattered and one was blown over a tree to a nearby field and so escaped; on the same day five prisoners taken from Killarney jail were brutally treated and four died. A few days later four prisoners on the way to jail were taken from the lorry and shot in a field. On 12 March, five prisoners met a similar fate. The conflict was now deteriorating into a bitter attack, such atrocities were unmatched by anything previously seen in an Irish conflict.

'Liam was nauseated by the news,' according to Todd Andrews. 'He seemed to live with the irradicable belief that Irish men, particularly if they had served in the pre-truce IRA, were born without the stain of original sin.'[5]

On 2 March, Lynch had directed the adjutant general (Con Moloney before capture) to call a meeting of the Executive for 9 a.m. on Thursday 15 March in the Second Southern Division area. Northern members were to assemble at Rathgormach, western members at the Glen of Aherlow and southern members at Araglin on the same date. It had been decided that all members would eventually go to the vicinity of Goatenbridge. However, because of continuous Free State activity in the area, arrangements had to be cancelled and the meeting was postponed until 23 March. De Valera had meanwhile written to Con Moloney (5 March) stating his disappointment that Lynch, 'has sent no report. His silence seems ominous to me. I think the former O/C Second Southern Division should proceed to that area and investigate the condition there.'[6]

During this period, while arrangements were being made for the holding of the Executive meeting, a proposal for the cessation of hostilities was being mooted by the archbishop of Cashel Dr Harty. A letter as well as a number of other proposals were mooted by priests and laymen who had contacted Tom Barry requesting that Republican leaders should be informed of the contents of the letter which was issued on 2 March.[7]

The idea behind the letter was to bring the sides together and 'end the present deplorable state of affairs in Ireland ...' Under three points there was a call for 'the immediate cessation of hostilities ... the dumping of arms ...' and 'subsequent to a General Election the arms and munitions to be handed over to the elected Government of the country.'[8]

Fr Tom Duggan was one of the main instigators in preparing the peace proposals and, at his request, Tom Barry agreed to circulate the document. On 15 March, Lynch, Barry and other officers of the First Southern Division were in the Ballyvourney district when Fr Duggan called on them and again spoke of some 'peace formula'. Lynch stuck to his views as set out in previous documents. Fr Duggan, still hopeful, left two days later for Dublin to meet Archbishop Byrne and W. T. Cosgrave, head of the Free State government. According to Todd Andrews, 'Barry was much more flexible; but Lynch made it clear to all that he was not willing to compromise in any way. There was a strongly worded letter to Barry which I saw, in which Lynch ordered him to discontinue further involvement in peace talks.'[9]

Lynch and Andrews were in bed one night when the bedroom door was suddenly kicked open. A figure appeared in the doorway holding a lighted candle in one hand and a sheet of paper in the other. Both men jumped up believing 'that we are at the mercy of the Staters.' Then Liam recognised Tom Barry.

Barry waved the piece of paper. 'Lynch, did you write this?' he shouted angrily.

'Yes,' Liam replied.

'A tirade of abuse followed from Barry, mainly directed at asserting the superiority of his fighting record.' The paper in Barry's hand was Liam's order to withdraw from peace feelers. Liam did not respond to Barry's abuse, but waited until 'having emptied himself of indignation, Barry withdrew slamming the door ...'

At night time, Lynch, who spoke little by day, would chat about the day's events or newspaper items which, according to Andrews, had become mere propaganda sheets for the Free State government. Lynch specifically resented the term 'irregulars' which was used by the Provisional Government and others to describe the anti-treaty forces. 'He often adverted to his beliefs that if we accepted the treaty we would become a mere province of Britain.' Andrews once ventured to suggest what a misfortune it was that the country had not given De Valera full control and stood by him in his rejection of the treaty. 'Liam didn't altogether agree with this view; even Document No. 2 would have been too much for him willingly to accept. Liam had not been at all in favour of the IRA setting up an alternative government; he believed that De Valera would make a compromise peace and he opposed the holding of a meeting of the Executive for the same reason'.[10]

Lynch, accompanied by Todd Andrews, left Gurteenflugh on 17 March for the Executive meeting which was to be held in Bliantas at the foot of the Monavullagh mountains. At Carriganimma they were joined by Tom Crofts, Tom Barry, Humphrey Murphy and a number of other men.[11]

They were taken by lorry to Bweening, from there they travelled by pony and trap. 'Tom Barry immediately took command,' said Todd Andrews. 'We drove into the night and it was easy to see why Barry was probably the best field commander in the IRA. Before approaching any cross roads he dismounted, covering the passage of the lorry with the bodyguards. The operation he was commanding was not complicated, but his air of confidence and authority impressed me. One felt safe with Barry in charge.'[12] Around midnight they arrived outside Kilworth having decided previously to abandon the lorry and continue on foot towards Araglin. Feeling thirsty they decided to call on a pub, had one round, and moved off in three pony and traps provided by the local company to pre-arranged billets organised by these North Cork men.

Apparently 'the boys' had some days previously acquired a lorry-load of bacon and distributed it to the people around the area. Lynch, Barry and the others had a wholesome meal before trudging twenty miles over the Knockmealdowns to Ballinamult for the all-important Executive meeting – the meeting which the members had waited months for Lynch to convene.[13]

Death on the Knockmealdowns

The available Executive members assembled on 23 March 1923 at James Cullinane's, Bliantas. In view of the important matters to be discussed, De Valera, was also present.[1] Anxious to stop the war De Valera stated at the meeting that Irish sovereignty and the abolition of the oath were prerequisites. Following a discussion on the general situation, Tom Barry proposed that the Executive recognise that continued resistance would not further the cause of independence.

The meeting had to move into the Nire Valley on 25 March because of reports of raiding forces in the area. Here the session continued at John Wall's, Glenanore until 26 March. (This meeting took three days.)[2] No minutes are available, but captured documents of the proceedings were published in the *Irish Independent* of 9 April 1923. From this long conference three viewpoints emerged. The following is a summary:

(1) Lynch's decision was to continue to fight, despite losses or disaster, until opponents agreed to the conditions of negotiation. It was his belief that they were still capable of offering resistance to the imposition of the treaty and that it was their duty to do so. That point of view received little support.

(2) The belief was held that a continuation of the armed struggle was no longer the best means of advancing the cause of the Republic, and that it would be possible through negotiations with the Free State government to agree to certain principles which would leave the Irish people uncommitted to the Treaty, and Republicans free to advance their cause without restriction. In principle, this meant that it would be possible for the Republicans to participate in the political and parliamentary life of the nation without taking the oath of allegiance to a foreign monarch.

(3) The view was held that the Free State authorities were unwilling to negotiate despite the maximum military effort which had been made, and had failed. Therefore, the war should be ended, thus saving further sacrifice of lives in the cause of the Republic. This view advocated the dumping of arms as the most acceptable way of ending the resistance.

These main points were discussed in view of:

1: The heavy losses by death and capture of officers and men.
2: The executions which had again been resumed in March following their suspension in February.
3: Lack of arms and ammunition to continue with further resistance.

It was estimated that, at this time, internment camps held approximately 13,000 prisoners. There seemed to be no way that they could retaliate against the execution of men other than through anarchy and Lynch would not agree to this policy.

Though Michael Cremin had been negotiating the importation of arms from the continent, there was no indication that this would be successful. Lynch was more hopeful than the situation warranted that arms would be forthcoming from Germany. In December 1922 as chief-of-staff of the IRA, he had written to Joe McGarrity in the United States expressing the hope that 'you have by now met Comdt Gen. Seán Moylan who has been sent by Army Council as Executive Representative to Clan' for the purpose of collecting funds and negotiating the purchase of heavy weapons to be got through Germany and dispatched to Ireland.[3]

In a letter that Lynch had sent to Seán Moylan on 6 February 1923 it appears as if he was confident of obtaining at least 'one piece of artillery now ... which could be moved round amongst our strong force and this would completely demoralise enemy and end the war ... A big cargo is not required; even a few, with sufficient shells, would finish up the business here ...'[4] During this period Lynch appeared to live under the false hope that things would go his way – that arms would come, that all would be right for the Republicans and, therefore, for Ireland.

A proposition at the March Executive meeting, formulated and proposed by Tom Barry and seconded by Tom Crofts suggested:

That in the opinion of the Executive further armed resistance and operations against F. S. government will not further the cause of independence of the country.

As this motion (which De Valera was not allowed to vote on, but was allowed to speak in its favour)[5] was defeated by one vote, five against six (Lynch voting against the motion),[6] it appeared impossible to reconcile the divergent views held by members of the Executive. Because of this, and also the hope that mountain artillery would soon become available, a decision was taken to adjourn the meeting until 10 April. Meanwhile, De Valera was to endeavour to bring certain negotiations which had been progressing through intermediaries to finer points so that they could be presented at the next Executive meeting, which would re-assemble at Araglin.

After the meeting, Lynch walked down the road with De Valera. He reflected aloud 'I wonder what Tom Clarke would think of this decision.'[7]

De Valera stopped. 'Tom Clarke is dead,' he said. 'He has not our responsibilities. Nobody will ever know what he would do, for this situation did not arise for him. But it has risen for us and we must face it with our intelligence and conscious of our responsibility.'[8]

Southern members, Barry, Crofts, and McSwiney returned to the Ballyvourney area while Lynch, Aiken and Hyde moved northwards towards Callan. While billeted in Kilcash on Good Friday 30 March, Lynch received news that Matt Ryan, a member of his staff, had been killed the previous day. It was again a moment of soul-searching for Liam. When Kathleen Barry spoke to him, he said that there were three courses open to him: 'to fight on; to surrender; a third option – he would not mention as he did not like to contemplate – the dumping of arms.' But he told her that the adjourned Executive meeting would clarify the position. Even then, he had an optimistic faith in the ability of the western divisions to continue the fight. Lynch told Todd Andrews before they parted a few days earlier, that 'he hoped he would be able to carry the Executive with him in his determination to fight on ... he had hopes of making a comeback in the west' and had suggested that after the Executive meeting he would send

Andrews to the west 'to take charge there'.

Lynch, at this stage, wished to visit Kirwans of Graigavalla where he had billeted while on the run after action in Fethard in September 1919. He wanted to be with Bridie Keyes. It was the last time she would see him alive. It was a very memorable visit; the Republic's cause was foremost in most of the conversations; as Liam's boots were pretty worn, Jerry Kirwan took it upon himself to repair them. (These are now in the National Museum, Dublin.)

Liam bid Bridie and the rest a last farewell. Afterwards they would all recall this visit as he left them and headed for Jim O'Brien's of Poulacappal, which was approximately four miles south-west of Callan. A number of local people had helped O'Brien to build a most unusual hide-out which housed most of the important Republican leaders during the Civil War – men like Tom Barry, Liam Deasy, De Valera and of course Lynch himself. It was christened 'Katmandu'.

'Katmandu' was a room about ten by five concealed at the end of a cow shed on the farm of the brothers Michael and John Phelan. The building had corrugated-iron walls and a roof partly covered with corrugated iron and partly thatched. Access to the hide-out was through this cow shed. The opening to it was cleverly constructed and could only be opened by anyone who knew the secret. The bunk-style bed-board would hold up to fourteen men, and in a corner stood a hinged-table where many important historical documents were signed. (On one occasion, twelve men including Liam held their breaths inside while a search went on outside.)

It was now Easter 1923. Liam had his meals at Gardiner's but he worked and slept at 'Katmandu'.[9] Despite the very serious position of the Republican forces, as outlined at the last Executive meeting, Liam was determined to continue the struggle in the field and to use his policy of armed resistance until, he believed, his opponents would be forced to negotiate.

Accompanied by Frank Aiken and Seán Hyde he left 'Katmandu' on 4 April 1923 on the first leg of the journey towards Araglin. In a pony and trap Jim O'Brien brought them to Nine-Mile House and they continued southwards to the Suir which they crossed west of Carrick, joined the old route and went through the Gap into the Nire Valley where they rested at Wall's of Knockaree and were joined next day by Bill Quirke, Seán O'Meara and Seán Hyde.

By Sunday midnight on 8 April, they had come into the sixth battalion area of the Third Tipperary brigade near Goatenbridge. That night, while Liam was billeted at Prendergast's, Owen McCarthy, a dispatch rider, brought a report from Araglin that over the next few days they could expect a round up in the locality. Liam felt that it was now wiser not to continue towards Araglin, so he sent the dispatch rider with these instructions to the rest of the Executive.

Lynch and his companions, fearful that death could be around any turn, moved again that night towards the banks of the Tar River; he stayed with Frank Aiken and Seán Hyde at Michael Condons; James Condon and Bill Houlihan housed the others.[10]

Before dawn on Tuesday 10 April, reports came from the scouts at Croke schoolhouse of the sighting of Free State troops – moving in two files along the grass margins on either side of the road, approaching from the Clogheen direction. Lynch and his group having been alerted, had assembled by 5 a.m. at Bill Houlihans, which was the house nearest the mountains. Raids of this nature were an everyday occurrence; they felt they had left no tell-tale marks so they were willing to sit it out and were not unduly ruffled.

At about 8 a.m. a scout rushed in saying that another column of Free State troops was approaching over the mountain to their left. Their line of escape was being threatened. Leaving Bill Houlihans they dashed up a glen towards the mountain. Lynch and five officers, armed with revolvers and automatics, and an unarmed local volunteer, struggled through the gorse. At the head of the glen they waited momentarily for the two scouts who were armed, one with a Thompson and the other a rifle. Maurice Twomey, one of the officers records:

> We were only a few minutes at the head of the glen, with no sign of the scouts coming when the Staters' appeared over a rise and our first shots were exchanged. We dashed on again, up the mountain, a shallow river-bed affording us cover for about 250 yards. When we reached the end of the river-bed we had to retreat up a bare coverless shoulder of mountain. This was the 'Staters' chance. About fifty of them had a clear view of us at between 300 and 400 yards range and they rattled away with their rifles as fast as they could work the bolts. Our return fire, with revolvers, was of course ineffective at that range; but as we staggered on up the mountain we fired an odd shot to disconcert their aim.[11]

Liam and his comrades continued to move up the rise of Crowhill. As they retreated over a bare shoulder of the Knockmealdown mountain they were aware of their exposed position but had no option. Then the Free State troops opened fire again. Fragments of rock and soil thrown up by the bullets rained on them as they struggled upwards. The men, all officers, walked or scrambled in single formation but kept going hoping to get to the other side of the mountain out of view of the Free State troops. 'Liam and Seán Hyde were to the rear. The "Staters" had fired over a thousand shots at us without effect, when a lull came in the firing.'[12]

After some seconds' silence, in the still clear air of the morning a single shot rang out. Liam fell. 'My God! I'm hit lads,' he said.[13]

Immediately Bill Quirke and Frank Aiken, who were in front of Liam, heard the call and rushed back. They picked him up, and with Seán Hyde who had been in the rear, carried him some distance. Hyde and Quirke took his arms and Frank Aiken lifted his legs and continued, but it was evident that he was in intense pain and he begged them to leave him. But they continued to carry him; and kept saying the act of contrition. Heavy fire from the Lewis gun knocked splinters off the large rock behind which they had taken temporary shelter. After a lull, when they again prepared to resume their journey, Liam asked them to leave him. Because of their reluctance he finally ordered them to put him down and go on. 'I'm finished,' he said, 'I'm dying. Perhaps they'll bandage me when they come up.' His companions realised it was the end. Hyde and Quirke pillowed a coat behind his head and reluctantly left him. Frank Aiken took his papers and his automatic, said another act of contrition as his life was slowly ebbing, put a coat over him then bade a final quick farewell to his friend as their enemy approached.[14]

Major General John T. Prout, Waterford commanding Free State officer with headquarters at Clonmel, had heard that certain Republican leaders were in the area, consequently he ordered a search of part of the South Tipperary and Waterford area to commence at dawn on 10 April. Over 1,000 troops were engaged in the search. Sixty men from Clogheen under Captain Tom Taylor and Lieut Laurence Clancy, arrived at Goatenbridge at 5 a.m. This was the party which had been observed by the scouts. Taylor had instructed his troops to drive south-east from Newcastle at dawn in a well extended formation across the mountain towards Ballymacarbery where they would link up with another column. Taylor's troops marched to Newcastle extended in formation up the mountain and then broke into two parts. It was the section under Lieut Clancy who saw Liam Lynch and his men and opened fire on them.

When Lieut Clancy reached Liam, the soldier who had been covering him with a rifle shouted excitedly, 'We've captured De Valera.' Clancy knew at first glance that he was mistaken. When he looked down on the helpless prisoner he asked, 'Are you the bloody chief-of-staff of the Irregulars?'

'I am Liam Lynch, chief-of-staff of the Irish Republican Army. Get me a priest and doctor. I'm dying.'

'Where are your guns?' asked Clancy who proceeded to search him.

'My friends have taken my guns,' he answered, and then gave
a painful moan.

Clancy gave a quick search to confirm that he didn't have a
gun, and then asked where he had been hit. When Clancy
looked for a field bandage, one of his soldiers refused to give 'a
diehard' the one he was wearing. 'I was compelled to produce my
revolver to get the bandage ... which was totally inadequate for
Lynch's body, and he was suffering pain.'[15]

A stretcher was improvised by tying a soldier's greatcoat to
two rifles: then began the difficult task of carrying Liam down
the steep and rugged mountainside. 'It was extremely difficult to
try to keep a big heavy man on two rifles, three feet eight inches
long, and in a semi-sitting position, because he could not bear to
be fully stretched with his wound,' said Lieut Clancy. In this half
sitting position he was able to endure the intense pain. Frequently he had to be rested as he was getting weaker.

Liam was placed on a jennet and a cart filled with hay when
they reached the foot of the mountain. Over the rough by-roads
this mode of transport was little better for the severely wounded
chief-of-staff. A disarmed soldier, whom Clancy had sent to secure a priest and doctor had panicked upon reaching the road;
fearing that he would encounter some Republican forces he turned
back. Shortly afterwards, however, Fr Patrick Hallinan, Newcastle, came along. The priest was unaware of what had happened
but gladly administered the last rites to Liam Lynch.

It was now about 11.30 a.m. Liam had received the bullet
wound around 9 a.m. In great pain he was carried over the rugged
road and reached Nugent's public house in Newcastle around
1.30 p.m. Here Liam was put on a sofa, some blankets were
placed over him, and he was given a glass of brandy. Dr Joseph
Power attended to his wounds while the local parish priest, Fr
John Walsh, came and prayed. Neighbours, who had gathered in
the parlour, responded to the rosary, which was recited by Fr
Walsh as two blessed candles flickered on the walls and on anxious faces.

Meanwhile Lieut Clancy had phoned his headquarters in Clonmel, reported the capture and asked for a doctor and ambulance. As they waited, Liam, in a faint voice, said to Lieut Clancy, 'When I die tell my people I want to be buried with Fitzgerald in Fermoy ... the greatest friend I have had.'

Clancy told him he had two brothers killed during the War of Independence, and that he himself had been arrested. Liam raised his right hand, and his eyes were filled with tears. 'With my hand clasped in his, I too sobbed,' said Clancy. With some difficulty Liam spoke: 'God pray for me. All this is a pity. It should never have happened. I am glad now I am going from it all. Poor Ireland. Poor Ireland!'[16]

Liam was not a man to bear any malice in life, nor now as he lay dying in enemy hands. He told Clancy what to do with the few possessions he had on him and told him to keep his silver fountain pen 'for the way you treated me. God bless you and the boys who carried me down the hill. I am sorry for all the trouble I caused you and them.'[17] (Lieut Clancy later handed over the pen with the other possessions and instructions on what was to be done with them; he asked General Prout to return the pen to him after the inquest. Clancy alleged this was not done.)

It was 3.15 p.m. when the ambulance arrived. Liam was then taken to St Joseph's Hospital, Clonmel, where he received good medical attention. But by this time he had lost too much blood and was bleeding internally.

At 8.45 p.m. that evening he died.

Over the next few days the uncovered oak coffin rested in the mortuary of St Joseph's church giving an opportunity for those who could, to pay their respects.

When his fiancée Bridie Keyes approached the coffin, she stood and looked on him. Then she held his hand and stroked his face. Her friend said that her tears were within. 'She did not cry. Her eyes just glazed. She froze. She never expected Liam would get shot, he was such a determined person, and so strong. Bridie had a belief that he was invincible.' Bridie moved from the locality sometime after Liam's death. She worked in the Irish Hospital Sweepstakes' office, and it is understood, she never married.

Soldiers of the Free State army and members of the Cumann na mBan guarded the body by night and day. Free State officers kept a watching brief on those who filed past. Because of this, many of his former comrades in arms were unable to offer a last farewell to their comrade and *Chief*.

Liam Lynch, chief-of-staff of the IRA in an open coffin, with Bridie Keyes, his fiancée, on the left and on the right his mother, Mary Lynch
(Courtesy, Christy O'Callaghan)

Inquest and final resting

Liam Lynch's death, at first glance, poses no question as the bullet, which hit him was a supposedly long-range shot from the opposing forces. So why should its source be questioned?

Doubtless his death came during a delicate stage of negotiations and at a time when ostensibly he was unprepared to compromise, therefore it appears that, mainly with hindsight, speculation entered into discussions on the original source of the fatal bullet. Thus the question posed is whether the bullet which took Liam Lynch's life was fired by the enemy or by a member of his accompanying party. Was the execution of the fatal shot masterminded by Republicans since he was by this time a stumbling block in any peace negotiations?

Maurice Twomey, in an interview in *An Phoblacht* stated:

> Our line of retreat was thus threatened and sending word to the scouts watching to the west we dashed up a glen towards the mountains. On reaching the head of the glen we halted to wait for the two scouts who were armed, one with a Thompson and the other with a rifle ... We were carrying a great number of important papers which we wished to save at all costs.

Just before he was hit Seán Hyde had been helping him 'as he had been nearly exhausted with the run up the river-bed.'

Twomey said:

> Our agony in the parting with our leader and Chief is something we could not easily describe ... The man who beat Strickland to the ropes died as he wished on an Irish mountain, fighting ... Who can explain why he, to save whom every man in the Republican army would have died, was killed, and not one of those who escaped? As we ran on again the ground round us was being spattered with bullets as thick almost as a shower of hail stones ...[1]

Frank Aiken later told Ned Murphy (Free State intelligence officer) that even though they knew Lynch was badly wounded they thought they'd get him away. 'We had almost reached the top of the difficult climb. Indeed just before he was hit we felt we could put on speed as we had the rugged climb over us '

Frank Aiken wrote:

> It would be impossible to describe our agony of mind in thus parting with our comrade and *Chief*. Even in the excitement of the fight we knew how terrible was the blow that had fallen on the nation and army on being deprived of his leadership. His command that we should leave him would have been disobeyed, but that the papers we carried must be saved and brought through at any cost. All would be lost if they were captured.[2]

The documents concerned peace formulas, surrender terms, together with hide-outs, importation of arms, contacts, flexible headquarters, and several other important private documents.

Seán Hyde recalled, 'The bullet which got him whizzed past me. There were several times when each one of us came close to being hit, earth and bushes splashed around us. There was one occasion when a blast of gunfire rained rocks and soil along an area between us and the boys in front.' He had no doubt but that the fatal shot came from the road below. 'Unless you have been through the ordeal it is difficult for another person to understand the heart-tug of taking a final look at a friend, a great man, a great leader, our *Chief* whom we knew was dying; we had no option but to leave him which meant he would shortly be in enemy hands.'[3]

The available records do not mention whether or not De Valera had arrived for the meeting and would therefore be compelled to retreat up the mountains with the others.

Newspaper reports state that Lynch, when captured, is understood to have stated that De Valera had made good his escape.[4]

General Prout in an interview said that a young man was lying face upwards in a thick growth of mountain shrubbery, he was dangerously wounded.[5] His clothes were thickly stained with blood and he was bleeding from the lower part of the body.

The *Irish Independent* reported:

> The news of the capture, says our correspondent, created great ex-

citement in Clonmel, which was intensified when it became known that Mr De Valera had narrowly avoided capture. According to the facts available in Clonmel yesterday afternoon troops advancing over the country at the foot of the Knockmealdown mountain in Newcastle-Ballybacon district were fired on. The troops returned the fire and Liam Lynch was captured, severely wounded. Several other leaders, including Mr De Valera and Dan Breen escaped ... When Liam Lynch was wounded his companions tried to carry him away, but owing to the hot pursuit of the troops they parted, and he was captured ... At the spot where he was wounded in the mountain, troops found top boots and hats belonging evidently to his companions.[6]

Certainly Dan Breen was not in the party, and all the evidence points to the fact that De Valera was not in the vicinity, though at the March meeting he had indicated his intention of being present at this assembly. Confusion seems to have arisen because of the similarity of the two men – both tall and slim and wearing glasses. On 9 April 1923, the day when members of the Executive were making their way towards the foot of the Knockmealdowns for the all-important meeting, De Valera wrote to P. J. Ruttledge:

To me our duty seems plain, to end the conflict without delay ... The phase begun in 1916 has run its course ... Those who would continue working for our independence must gird themselves for a long patient effort of reorganisation, and education.[7]

On 10 April 1923, as the Executive members had assembled at Houlihan's for the meeting and were forced to flee to the Knockmealdowns, De Valera wrote to Austin Stack:

The decision lies between 'a quit' by a governmental proclamation and army order to 'cease fire', or a public pronouncement by the Government of the basis on which it is prepared to make peace.[8]

Dr Stokes, deputy coroner, held an inquest on the remains at Clonmel Union Boardroom, on 11 April. A military witness, Colonel Jerry Ryan identified the body as 'that of Liam Lynch a native of Anglestabo, Co. Limerick, who was aged about 33 years, single. I knew he took an active part in the operations against the government forces and I believe he was Chief-of-Staff of the Irregulars.'[9] (He was in fact 29 years of age.)

Captain T. Taylor stated he was 'in charge of a column operating in Crohane Mountain and about 10 a.m. yesterday fire was opened on us by a number of Irregulars. The party returned the fire. Firing lasted about half an hour. My party proceeded under fire and the Irregulars retreated. We found a man wounded face upwards. One of my party attended to him and had his wounds dressed ... We took him down from the mountain to Newcastle where he was attended by a priest and Dr Power, Ardinane. Dr Dalton soon arrived with a Red Cross ambulance ... The wounded man had no arms on him when we found him.'[10]

Dr Redmond Dalton, military MO, stated he went out with an ambulance to Newcastle and found Liam Lynch in a house. 'There were two bullet wounds in the body, one the entrance wound, being somewhat behind and to the right, between the lower border of the ribs and hip. The exit wound was at the about the same level on the left side. There was a fair amount of external and a considerable amount of internal haemorrhage, and he was suffering very severely from shock. After consultation with the doctor who was attending the patient, we decided it was best that he should be removed to Clonmel. We brought him back in the ambulance arriving about 6 o'clock in the military ward, St Joseph's Hospital. The patient was very low all the time, and died shortly before 9 o'clock. Death was due to shock and haemorrhage following the wounds described.'

The jury, after a brief consultation, found that 'death was due to shock and haemorrhage due to bullet wounds caused by a party of the National Army in the execution of their duty. The coroner joined with the Jury in the expression of sympathy with the relatives.'[11]

Free State intelligence officer Ned Murphy said one of their soldiers saw movement of men 'and aimed at one of them, he was aware that he had hit a man; this turned out to be Lynch.' Murphy was confident from their internal army questioning, that in a war situation an enemy had been hit, and the query that the bullet originated from any source 'other than from a national army rifle should not arise.'

At the inquest there seemed to be no doubt but that the fatal bullet was a long-range shot fired from a national army weapon, and admitted to, by them – and to imply that a bullet came from any other source would be mere speculation.

At the inquest a juror stated that the jury would like to know if the last wish of deceased (that he be buried in Fermoy) would be carried out. The coroner responded that General Prout had 'given an assurance as to that already.'

On the night of 10 April, news of Liam's death was telegraphed to Willie Ryan in Mitchelstown who immediately travelled with Mrs Hyland to Liam's mother in Barnagurraha.

Sorrow was obviously written on their faces because as soon as they arrived, she said, 'He is dead, Willie,' then paused momentarily. 'Thank God he did not let down his comrades!' Over the next few days, in the ordeal which followed, she bore her grief silently and, publicly at least, her tears remained unshed.

Liam's brother, Jack who was in Maryboro jail said with sadness to John Flanagan that night, 'I always felt he'd go by the bullet.'

Some former comrades (now with the opposing forces) suggested, according to newspaper reports, that Liam Lynch should be dressed in the full uniform of a volunteer officer; also amongst the thousands of people who visited the hospital and filed in 're-spectful silence past the bier were numbers of soldiers of the national army and members of the civic guard.'[12]

On Thursday morning Liam's brother, Bro. Martin with Mary MacSwiney, 'Mrs Kate O'Callaghan, T.D. widow of the former Mayor of Limerick, Count Plunkett, T.D. [and] a Mr McCarthy of Limerick … were passing through Tipperary by train on their way to Clonmel for Liam Lynch's funeral', the *Cork Examiner* reported. 'Military boarded the train and placed the party under arrest. Mary MacSwiney refused to leave the train, and eventually the military released Liam Lynch's brother and re-moved the others to the local military headquarters. Mr Lynch's brother was not interfered with and proceeded to his destination.'[13]

The body of the dead leader remained in view in St Joseph's church, Clonmel, until Friday morning when members of the family came to attend mass. 'Brother [Martin] Lynch betrayed great emotion as he looked down on the pale features of his dead brother ... his mother bore with apparent resignation the death of her son.'[14]

The remains were removed from St Joseph's church mortuary, Clonmel, to Mitchelstown. The lying-in-state continued during the day and up to the last moment hundreds of people visited the church to file past the coffin. The *Irish Independent* reports that three bands of gold braid were attached to the sleeves of the uniform in which the body was garbed:[15]

> There was a heart-rending scene just before the removal, when the aged mother, sister, and brothers of the dead leader took their final farewell of their loved one. The only sound to break the stillness of the death-chamber was the loud sobbing of the bereaved ones, and many present were moved to tears.
>
> The coffin was then draped in a huge tricolour with mourning crosses, and on the lid were placed the deceased's belt and cap ... The remains were carried from the hospital by a number of the deceased's comrades. Just outside the building the military guard turned out, and as the coffin bearing the remains passed by, the men presented arms at the word of command from an officer, and remained in that position until all the mourners had passed.[16]

Though Civil War was still dominating people's views, all the shops and business premises suspended their activities 'during the passage of the funeral. In practically all the houses blinds were drawn. Large crowds assembled all along the footpaths.'

As the cortege passed by the post office 'the military guard there also turned out and presented arms. On the outskirts of the town the remains were placed in a motor hearse for conveyance to Mitchelstown.' The *Irish Independent* reports:

> Another touching tribute was here paid by the file of civic guards,

who lined along the road, and as the hearse passed by they stood to attention and saluted.

The remains were then conveyed to Mitchelstown.

For a considerable time before the remains were removed from the Mitchelstown church, people began to assemble amidst heavy rain in the square and thoroughfares adjoining the church, and by the time that the funeral started on its journey the gathering had assumed huge proportions.

'The coffin surrounded by the tricolour, and on which had been laid deceased's volunteer cap and belt, was borne on the shoulders of his comrades from Mitchelstown, around the principal streets of the town before being placed in a hearse and conveyed to the cemetery.'[17]

Despite the conflict raging in a bitter civil war, friend and foe followed the cortege along the route as the body of Liam Lynch was carried through Glanworth and Fermoy to Kilcrumper. Crowds lined the countryside and towns for the final farewell to the man, who like his friend, comrade and fellow Cork man Michael Collins, met his death in a Cork hillside in the war of brothers – the sad irony of Ireland's history.

The church bells at Mitchelstown and Fermoy rang out simultaneously as his dying wish was fulfilled when he was laid beside his friend and comrade, Michael Fitzgerald.

Professor Stockley, TD, who delivered the oration, said, 'Ireland should be allowed to live her own life, and it was in that hope Mr Lynch had lived and died...'[18]

> The number of horse vehicles was not less than 300, and when the cortege left Mitchelstown for the cemetery, it stretched along the road a distance of about five miles. The remains had been interred and all the last rites concluded before thousands of people could have reached the cemetery.[19]

The surviving officers and men of the army he had led so fearlessly could not come to pay a last tribute to their dead *Chief*, but wherever they were scattered – whether on the hillside, in the towns or in hiding, in jails or internment camps like his brother Jack – their hearts were with him in Kilcrumper.

Among the many wreaths was one, which bore the inscription: *When Emmet's epitaph shall be written, Ireland will write yours, Liam. – Éamon de Valera.*[20]

In the centre, Bridie Keyes, Liam's fiancée, and on the right, Mrs Mary Lynch pictured with friends at a Liam Lynch anniversary commemoration
(Courtesy, Christy O'Callaghan)

The 60 foot high round tower on the Knockmealdowns marks the spot where Liam Lynch was shot. Designed by Denis Doyle, unveiled 7 April 1935, by Maurice Twomey ('on the run' at the time). Brian O'Higgins' oration was delivered before an estimated 15,000 people
(Courtesy, Christy O'Callaghan)

Appendix I

The agreement between Commandant General Hannigan and
General Liam Lynch was signed at 6.30 on 4 July 1922

'AGREED'

Commandant General Hannigan will not at any time attack the Executive forces; Executive forces will not attack Commandant General Hannigan's forces.

The Executive forces will not occupy any posts in East Limerick Brigade area.

That both sides only occupy their normal number of posts in Limerick city.

That there be no movement of armed troops in Limerick city or in East Limerick Brigade area, except by Liaison Agreement.

That Commandant General Hannigan withdraws any of his troops drafted into Limerick City since Saturday.

Executive communications to be maintained between 1st, 2nd and 3rd Southern Divisional Headquarters and Limerick City.

This agreement to hold during the period of fighting between Executive forces and Beggars' Bush or until both sides of the army find a solution to the problem.

We agree to these conditions in the practical certainty that national peace and unity will eventuate from our efforts, and we guarantee to use every means in our power to get this peace.

This agreement shall be put into effect by 12 o'clock tonight.

Appendix II

Striving to maintain the highest standard of efficiency in the columns, and taking account of successes and failures, Liam Lynch issued a number of memoranda. The following are samples taken from Operations Orders:

Operation Order 2 – 22/7/1922.

When resting, scouts or sentries should be posted on vantage points commanding a view of the whole country about. At night they should be posted on all roads, and should be provided with horns (or sounders) to signal the approach of the enemy.

When moving, Columns should have advanced and rear guards connected with the main body.

Columns should never move into country until it is first scouted and the O/C has satisfied himself that it is either free of the enemy, or is aware of the exact position he occupies.

Operation Order 9 – 19/8/1922.

They should keep close touch with one another. This is most necessary both from the point of view of co-operation in operations and of protecting one another from surprise or attack by the enemy ... Each unit while at rest should however provide independently for its own protection.

Each operation, no matter how simple it may appear, should be carefully planned, every detail attended to and all contingencies as far as possible provided against ...

Before going into action men should have clearly explained to them: (a) the objective to be achieved; (b) the line of retreat; (c) position of HQ and of different sections or units operating.

The strictest discipline on the part of the troops on active service must be insisted on, and any breaches of same should be promptly and sternly dealt with ... Officers should set a good example in the matter of discipline.

Appendix III

Proclamation Óglaigh na h-Éireann

WHEREAS this Junta called the 'Government of the Irish Free State', have suppressed the legitimate Parliament of the nation and usurped the government, and now, in the endeavour to make good their usurpation and to destroy the Republic, have resorted to the infamous practice of shooting Republican soldiers taken by them as prisoners of war, and have already put to death fifty-three Officers and Men in this manner.

AND WHEREAS, the Army of the Republic is determined that it will no longer suffer its members to be thus dealt with, and the international usage of war violated with impunity,

AND WHEREAS, the army Command of the said Junta, have issued a Proclamation announcing the 'Punitive Action' will be taken by them against other prisoners in their power if the hostages which we have been compelled to take are not set at liberty.

NOW, WE HEREBY GIVE NOTICE that we shall not give up our hostages, and if the threatened action be taken, we shall hold every member of the said Junta and its so-called Parliament, Senate and other House, and all their Executives responsible, and shall certainly visit them with the punishment they shall deserve.

DATED, this 1st day of February, 1923, at the hour of noon.

Liam Lynch, General,
Chief-of-Staff.
Field General H.Q., Dublin.

Appendix IV

Operation Order issued by Major-General John J. Prout, Officer Commander, Waterford Command, Emmet Barracks, Clonmel – to all units of the National Forces about to take part in this operation in the early hours of the morning of April 10, 1923.

(The O/C Clogheen garrison, received copy.)

Map Ref: Templemore and Tipperary sheet 22. Reliable information to hand. Important Irregular leaders are at present in South Tipperary or Waterford.

Objective:
It is the intention of the G.O.C. to surround that area and capture, if possible, or at least harass the enemy. All farm houses, out-houses, woods, mountains and likely hiding places will be thoroughly searched. Starting points and objectives, at conclusion, giving right and left flank Units or otherwise, columns from Clonmel, Tipperary, Cahir, Mitchelstown, Clogheen, Carrick-on-Suir and Dungarvan will take part.

No. X column from Clogheen under Captain Tom Taylor and one officer, together with sixty other ranks, will proceed at 04.00 hours from Clogheen and reach the village of Newcastle, Clonmel, not later than daybreak tomorrow, April 10, 1923.

At dawn you will drive out from Newcastle in a south-easterly direction with your troops in well extended formation. Search all farmsteads and other likely places across the Knock-mealdown Mountains and foothills, holding a well extended line across the mountain, Ballymacarbery, Mount Melleray right and left respectively, where you will link up with a column from Dungarvan operating in a north-westerly direction.

[N.B. This order was issued in the 'early hours of the morning' of 10th April, 1923, the day Liam Lynch was shot.]

Notes

The fatal shot

1. Letter to his brother, Tom, 1/11/1917 (Lynch private family papers)
2. One prisoner, representing each province: Rory O'Connor, Liam Mellows, Dick Barrett, Joe McKelvey.
3. Brigade Adjutant, First Southern Division. Liam Deasy, private papers.
4. John A. Murphy, Ireland in the Twentieth Century, p. 57. See also Eoin Neeson, The Civil War in Ireland, p. 190. Following the execution of four Republican prisoners (8 December 1922) as a reprisal for the shooting of Seán Hales (7 December 1922), Cosgrave announced in the Dáil that government policy 'was one of terror meeting terror'. The last official pro-treaty execution took place on 2 May 1923; see also MacEoin, Survivors, p. 88.
5. Letter to 'Comrades', 9 February 1923.
6. Seán Hyde, author interview, 13/7/1974.
7. Maurice Twomey.

Early life and vision of Ireland

1. Other members (seven children): Jeremiah who was accidentally drowned in London in 1904; James – died aged 39 of a clot after an operation; Martin – Christian brother died in Kilrush 1964; John remained on the home farm; Tom – priest went to Australia – Very Rev. Dean Lynch PP of Bega, New South Wales, died in Sydney 28 March, 1950; Margaret married locally.
2. 'I always thought Sarsfield made a daring ride ... Yes, but he burned the guns' – letter to his brother, Tom 15/11/1919 (Lynch private family papers).
3. Lynch private family papers.
4. Letter to his brother, Tom, 10/10/1917 (Lynch private family papers).

Declaration for an Irish Republic

1. Letter to Tom, 1/11/1917 (Lynch private family papers).
2. Letter to Tom, 9/11/1917 (Lynch private family papers).
3. Ibid.
4. Fermoy Battalion – Fermoy, Kilworth, Araglin, Rathcormac, Watergrasshill, Glenville, Ballynoe, Bartlemy, and Castlelyons.
5. Vol. 1., No. 2., September 1918.
6. Twenty Battalions with an average of eight companies each, and a total strength of about 8,000 men made up the brigade.
7. Cork No. 1 was in the centre extending from Youghal to the Kerry border beyond Ballyvourney and including the city; Cork No. 3 was in the west of the county, and Cork No. 2 in the north of the county.
8. The brigade area extended from the Cork/Waterford border near Tallow, on the east, to the Kerry border at Rathmore in the west and from Milford in the north almost to Donoghmore in the south.

Once the brigade was formed George Power, adjutant began to build up an intelligence service.
9   Lynch private family papers.

Love and marriage postponed for Roisín Dubh
1. Paddy O'Brien, author interview, 6/8/75; Matt Flood, author interview, 28/3/80; Florence O'Donoghue, *No Other Law*, p. 40.
2. Letter to Tom 9/11/1917 (Lynch private family papers).
3. Letter to Tom 6/3/1922 (Lynch private family papers).
4. Interview with Siobhán Creedon Langford; also Siobhán Creedon Langford, *The Hope and the Sadness*.

Military activity continues
1. Johnie Fanning, author interview, 12/6/1979.
2. In his brigade area British forces had approximately five battalions, two brigades of Royal Field Artillery; a machine gun battalion and two enemy brigade headquarters and staff. Total military garrison in his area not less than 4,300 all ranked; also approximately 490 armed police distributed in 54 posts mainly in the towns and villages throughout the brigade area.
3. Four men with George Power from Mallow Company – Owen Harold, Brian Kelly, Dan Hegarty and Ned Waters. They pretended they were on a Sunday trip to Mount Melleray.
4. Pat Leahy, John Joe Hogan, Peter O'Callaghan and Tom Griffin.
5. Driver of Buick – Leo O'Callaghan.
6. Larry Condon, Mick Fitzgerald, John Fanning, Ned Lane and William Lane took the rifles and transferred them to a dump in the Araglin area the following night.
7. Jim Keogh, Mick Kelleher and Michael Walshe.

Talks with Michael Collins and GHQ
1. Others arrested were James Fanning, John Swaine, John Joe Hogan, Martin O'Keeffe, Dick O'Keeffe, Pat Leahy, Tom Griffin, Peter O'Callaghan and Jack Mulvey.
2. Public Records Office, the British Library Board Newspaper Library.
3. Dan Hegarty, the brigade vice-commandant, then under arrest, was replaced by George Power; Maurice Twomey, then adjutant of Fermoy battalion, became brigade adjutant. Tom Barry, Glanworth, the brigade quartermaster, elected O/C of the Third Battalion, Castletownroche was replaced by Jeremiah Buckley, Mourne Abbey – arrested August 1920 replaced by Paddy O'Brien, Liscarroll – assistant Michael O'Connell.
4. Letter to Tom, 28/3/1920 – address at the head of the letter was 'County Cork' (Lynch private family papers).
5. Sir Nevil Macready, *Annals of an Active Life*, p. 241.
6. Dorothy Macardle, *The Irish Republic*, pp. 332, 333.

Arrested with Tomás MacCurtain
1. Sir Nevil Macready, *Annals of an Active Life*, Vol. 2, p.428.
2. Letter to Tom – torn fragment. A letter to his mother, 1/8/1921 contains similar sentiments: 'I would not wish to be born in any other generation but this. It is glorious to live at the present day ...' (Lynch private family papers).
3. An *tÓglach*, 1 May 1920.
4. Terence MacSwiney, Lord Mayor of Cork, TD for mid-Cork and commandant of Cork No. 1 Brigade. He became Lord Mayor of Cork after his friend and colleague, Tomás MacCurtain had been murdered.

Hostilities intensify – death of a true friend
1. An *tÓglach*, 1 July 1921.
2. Ammunition was found in Fitzgerald's house by the British forces and he was sentenced to two months imprisonment, released end of August, took part in Fermoy raid, 7 September 1919.

More comrades shot
1. Patrick McCarthy was arrested in 1918, took part in Belfast hunger-strike under Austin Stack and was transferred to Strangeways Jail, Manchester; escaped September 1919, returned to Ireland, joined the volunteers, involved in Mallow raid and all ambushes in the area.
2. Details of Kilmichael ambush in Meda Ryan, *The Tom Barry Story*, pp. 30–33.
3. Letter to his mother, 22/7/1921 (Lynch private family papers).

Intelligence
1. Order No 6, issued 4, June 1920.
2. Details in Siobhán Creedon Langford, *The Hope and the Sadness*, pp. 155,156.
3. Florence O'Donoghue, *No Other Law*, Chapter on 'Intelligence and Counter Intelligence', pp. 113–127.

Spies
1. Hundreds of men with British Army service loyally served in the IRA. His was an isolated case.

Formation of First Southern Division
1. The brigades represented were Cork No. 1; Cork No 2; Cork No. 3; Tipperary No. 2; Tipperary No. 3; East Limerick.
2. First formal conference, Southern Brigade, 6 January 1921
3. Ewan Butler, *Barry's Flying Column*.
4. Brigades: three Kerry, three Cork, two Waterford and one West Limerick.
5. Of these Cork No. 1 brigade with 7,500 all ranks was the largest; Cork No. 3 was next in strength with 5,270; Cork No. 2 numbered 4,700; Kerry No. 1 numbered 4,000; Kerry No. 2 numbered 3,400; Water-

ford (2 brigades) 2,270; West Limerick 2,100 and Kerry No. 3, 1,350. The British forces occupying the area were estimated at 11,260 including 18,750 troops, 1,600 RIC, 340 Auxiliaries, 570 marines.

6. At the meeting Cork No. 2 brigade was represented by Liam Lynch and Seán Moylan: Cork No. 1 by Seán O'Hegarty and Florence O'Donoghue: Cork No 3. by Liam Deasy and Tom Barry: and Cork No. 1 by Andy Cooney: Kerry No. 2 by Humphrey Murphy: Kerry No. 3 by John Joe Rice: Tipperary by Dan Breen: the Waterford and West Limerick brigades were not represented.

7. Meda Ryan, *The Tom Barry Story*, p. 77.

8. Ewan Butler, *Barry's Flying column*, p. 149.

GHQ's lack of consultation with Cork brigades.

1. Florence O'Donoghue, *No Other Law*, p. 160.

2. *Ibid.*, p. 161.

3. Operation Order No. 2, 22/7/1922.

4. *Ibid.*, No. 9. 19/8/1922. See Appendix II.

5. Meda Ryan, *The Tom Barry Story*, p. 99.

6. *The Morning Post*, 31/5/1921.

7. Tom Barry, *Guerrilla Days in Ireland*; also Meda Ryan, *The Tom Barry Story*.

8. Florence O'Donoghue, *No Other Law*, p. 177.

9. Piaras Beaslaí in *Michael Collins and the Making of a New Ireland*, stated 'Liam Lynch and other Southern IRA Officers went on a deputation to GHQ in Dublin to state that owing to the shortage of arms and ammunition and enemy pressure that they were unable to continue the fight.'

10. Tom Barry, *Guerrilla Days in Ireland*, pp. 170, 171.

11. See Meda Ryan, *The Tom Barry Story*, p. 74.

Truce – hope for full settlement

1. Brigadier-General F .P. Crozier, *Ireland Forever*, p. 91.

2. Sir Nevil Macready, *Annals of an Active Life*. Vol. 2, pp. 561–2.

3. *Diaries of Field Marshal Sir Henry Wilson*.

4. Major C. J. Street, (I.O.) *The Administration of Ireland, 1920*.

5. *An tÓglach*, March 1921.

6. Letter to his brother Tom, 6/9/1921 (Lynch private family papers).

Collins' offer – commander in-chief position

1. Letter to his brother Tom, Lombardstown 22/8/1921 (Lynch private family papers).

2. Letter to his brother Tom, 26/9/1921 (Lynch private family papers).

3. Matt Flood, author interview, 28/3/1980.

4. Letter to his brother Tom, Lombardstown, 26/8/1921 (Lynch private family papers).

5. See Frank Parkenham, *Peace by Ordeal*; also T. Ryle Dwyer, *Michael Collins and the Treaty*.

6. Letter to his brother Tom, 18/10/1921 (Lynch private family papers).
7. Mulcahy papers, University College, Dublin, Archives P7a/5. Cathal Brugha was minister for defence in December 1921. I could not find any written documentation of the offer.

IRB's allegiance to the Republic
1. Luby papers, National Library, MS 331.
2. Tom Hales and Pat Harte were tortured by the Essex squad having their fingernails pulled off and they were dragged for several miles after a lorry. Hales was kept in jail until after the treaty was signed. Harte went insane, was confined to an asylum and died a few years later.
3. S.C. 12/12/1921, The Organisation – Peace Treaty.
4. Florence O'Donoghue, No Other Law, p. 190.
5. Letter to his brother Tom, 12/12/1921 (Lynch private family papers).
6. Ibid., 12/12/1921 (Lynch private family papers).
7. Liam Deasy, Brother against Brother, p. 95. (Liam Deasy said subsequently that it would have been better if Liam Lynch had allowed Collins to state the true position to the meeting.)
8. Florence O'Donoghue, No Other Law, p. 192; also see Liam Deasy, Brother against Brother, p. 95.
9. Florence O'Donoghue, No Other Law, p. 192.
10. Letter to his brother Tom, 12/12/1921 (Lynch private family papers).
11. Letter to his brother Tom, 16/1/1922 (Lynch private family papers).
12. Liam Deasy author interview, 5/12/1972; Liam Deasy private papers.

First indication of treaty split
1. Paddy McCarthy having escaped from Manchester jail joined No. 2 brigade, took part in the Mallow episode, was killed in Millstreet two months later – being the first casualty in North Cork.
2. Irish Independent, 27 April 1922 (see next chapter, 'cancellation of Convention').

Army conventions – Executive chief-of-staff appointment
1. Published 12 March 1922.
2. Irish Independent, 27 April 1922. Lynch in a letter wrote 'the proposed Agreement ... was to select a Council of eight to frame definite proposals for associating the IRA with the new government elected by the Irish people ... was put before Mr Griffith and Mr Collins who turned down' that clause and decision to hold army convention. 'We then put the other clauses before the Divisional Council, and it was unanimously agreed not to put them before the meeting that evening ...'
3. Florence O'Donoghue, No Other Law, p. 219.
4. Mulcahy papers P7/B/192/60, University College, Dublin, Archives.
5. An official statement issued from the pro-treaty GHQ 5 April, challenged the representation at the convention to which Rory O'Connor replied in a lengthy statement (see the Irish Independent, 8 April 1922), saying that attention should be drawn to the fact that 'Dáil

Éireann did not object to the holding of a Convention as such: but to the defeat which the Minister for Defence foresaw.'

6. Any serving volunteer was eligible for election. (The convention nominated 25 members and gave them power to appoint the Executive)

7. Letter to his brother Tom, 18/4/1922 (Lynch private family papers).

8. Letter to his brother Tom, 6/3/1922 (Lynch private family papers).

9. British Public Records Office.

10. Letter to his brother Tom, 18/4/1922 (Lynch private family papers).

11. Mulcahy papers University College, Dublin. Archives, P7/B/192 – pages of atrocities. (Many events of lawlessness were alleged to have been undertaken by people who were not involved in any military conflict.)

Efforts for army unity

1. Mulcahy papers, University College, Dublin, Archives, P7/B/192/ 27 – Ten army officers: Dan Breen, H. Murphy, F. O'Donoghue, R. J. Mulcahy, Gearóid O'Sullivan, Tom Hales, S. O'Hegarty, Seán Boylan, Owen O'Duffy, Michael Ó Coileain.

2. Mulcahy papers, University College, Dublin, Archives, P7/B/192/ 71. Document agreed and signed, 1 May, 1922.

3. Mulcahy papers University College, Dublin, Archives, P7/B/192/ 19 – committee of ten: Seán Hales, Pádraig Ó Maille, Joseph McGuinness, Séamus O'Dwyer, Seán Mac Eoin, Mrs T. Clarke, Harry Boland, P. J. Ruttledge, Seán Moylan, Liam Mellows.

4. Mulcahy papers University College, Dublin, Archives, P7/B/192/ 26 and P7/B/192/29, also P7/B/192/301.

5. Mulcahy papers University College, Dublin, Archives, P7/B/192/ 301.

6. *Ibid.* P7/B/192/204.

7. *Ibid.* P7/B/193/211.

8. *Ibid.* P7/B/192/19.

9. *Ibid.* P7/B/192/72.

10. *Ibid.* P7/B/192/71.

11. *Ibid.* P7/B/192/196. In this letter O'Duffy expressed his opinion that he had hopes that the 'army situation would be settled by 1st July'.

12. Mulcahy papers, University College, Dublin, Archives P7/B/192/ 20.

13. Letter to his brother Tom, 18/4/1922 (Lynch private family papers).

Arms exchanged in northern offensive

1. Dan (Sando) O'Donovan (document – private papers).

2. Michael Farrell, *Irish Times*, 3 September 1982.

3. Others: Rory O'Connor, Liam Mellows, Seán MacBride, Tom Barry.

4. Michael Farrell, *Irish Times*, 14 December 1982.

5. Seán MacBride, author interview, 11/5/77; See also Seán MacBride, *Survivors*, p. 117 (editor, Uinseann MacEoin).

6. See also Pax O'Faolain, *Survivors*, p. 141.

7. Michael Farrell, *Irish Times*, 14 December 1982.

8. Florence O'Donoghue, *No Other Law*, p. 251.

9. Liam to his brother, Tom, 18/4/1922, (Lynch private family papers)

10. Liam to his brother Tom, 1/5/1922, (Lynch private family papers).
11. J. J. O'Connell papers – The National Library.
12. Michael Farrell, *Irish Times*, 14/12/1982.
13. Mulcahy papers, University College, Dublin, Archives, P7/B/193/7 also P7/B/192/301.
14. *Ibid.* P7/B/192/71.
15. *Ibid,* P7/B/192/72.
16. *Ibid.*
17. *Ibid.* P7/B/192/211.
18. Army Council: M/Defence, E. O'Duffy, L. Lynch, Seán Moylan, G. O'Sullivan, L. Mellows, R. O'Connor, F. O'Donoghue. GHQ Staff: chief-of-staff – Eoin O'Duffy; deputy chief-of-staff – Liam Lynch; deputy chief-of-staff – Liam Deasy; adj. general – Florence O'Donoghue; QMG – Seán McMahon; D/intelligence – G. O'Sullivan.
19. Previously Seán O'Hegarty, Tom Hales and Florence O'Donoghue had resigned on the issue of an attempt to forcibly prevent the holding of a general election – they were replaced by Tom Derrig, Tom Barry and Pax Whelan. See also Florence O'Donoghue, *No Other Law*, p. 245.
20. P7/B/192/157, Mulcahy papers, University College, Dublin, Archives.
21. *Melbourne Irish News* (Australia), 11 April 1924 (Lynch private family papers).
22. Lynch private family papers. Torn letter, date unknown.
23. Ernie O'Malley, *The Singing Flame*, p. 77
24. Seán MacBride, *Survivors*, 118.
25. *Ibid.*

Disunity and Civil War
1. Sir Nevil Macready, *Annals of an Active Life*. Vol. 2, pp. 652, 653.
2. Emmet Dalton, author interview, 20/3/1974.
3. Liam Deasy, author interview, 5/12/1972.
4. Florence O'Donoghue, *No Other Law*, p. 259. See also, Liam Deasy, *Brother against Brother*, p. 49.
5. C. Desmond Greaves, *Liam Mellows and the Irish Revolution*, p. 346.
6. Robinson brought his Tipperary men as far as Blessington where they joined up with the South Dublin brigade.
7. From the records it appears that Lynch did not see Prout and that the *War News*, statement was incorrect.
8. Paddy O'Brien, interview with author, 6/8/1975.
9. Florence O'Donoghue, also Paddy O'Brien collection, (Quoted: J. L. O'D 1/104/2.)

Compromise Limerick agreement
1. Connie Neenan, *Survivors*, p. 244
2. *Ibid.*
3. Liam Deasy, author interview, 5/12/1972.
4. Paddy O'Brien, author interview, 6/8/1975.
5. Mulcahy papers University College, Dublin, Archives, P7/B/192/ 173;

see also Eoin Neeson, *Civil War in Ireland*, pp. 88, 89; also Florence
O'Donoghue, *No Other Law*, pp. 262, 263.
6 See Appendix I.
7. P. G. 57 Minutes, 12 July 1922; also P7/B/244/38, Mulcahy papers, University College Dublin, Archives.
8. C. Desmond Greaves, *Liam Mellows and the Irish Revolution*, p. 357.
9. *Ibid*. p. 359.
10. Document captured at Blessington – Mulcahy papers, University College, Dublin Archives, P7/A/80.
11. Interview with Siobhán (Creedon) Langford, 6/9/1976; Siobhán Langford, *In Hope and in Sadness*, p. 241.

Memo on Michael Collins' death
1. Lynch private family papers.
2. *Ibid*. See also Mulcahy papers, File P7/B/2.
3. *Ibid*.
4. *Ibid*.
5. Operation Order No. 9, 19 August 1922.
6. Lynch private family papers.
7. *Ibid*.
8. Liam Lynch to Liam Deasy, 28 August, 1922, Deasy private papers. See
also, Eoin Neeson, *Sunday Review*, 11 January 1959.
9. Paddy O'Brien, author interview, 6/8/1975.
10. Liam Deasy, *Brother against Brother*.
11. Meda Ryan, *The Tom Barry Story*, p. 121.
12. Letters by Capt. T. C. Courtney to S. P. Cahalane – one of the intermediaries.
13. Mulcahy papers P7/D/65/22/20, University College, Dublin, Archives.
14. Ernest Blythe, author interview, 8/1/1974.
15. Emmet Dalton, author interview, 4/4/1974.
16. Letter by Lynch to his brother Tom, 27/10/1922 (Lynch private family
papers).
17. Lynch private family papers.
18. Florence O'Donoghue, *No Other Law*, p. 271.
19. Lynch private family papers.
20. Dorothy Macardle, *The Irish Republic*.
21. Longford and O'Neill, *Éamon De Valera*, p. 201.
22. Letter to his brother Tom, 28/10/1922 (Lynch private family papers).
23. HQ staff consisted of P. J. Ruttledge, Tom Derrig, Moss Twomey, Seán
Brunswick, Madge Clifford and Liam Lynch.
24. Mulcahy papers, University College, Dublin, Archives P7/A/199; See
also Florence O'Donoghue, *No Other Law*, p. 279.
25. Mulcahy papers, University College, Dublin, Archives P7/A/83.
26. Lynch private family papers, 22/12/1922.
27. Longford and O'Neill, *Éamon De Valera*, p. 212.

Determination and Hope of Victory

1. Ernest Blythe told me that they would continue until the last man was executed, if such became necessary, 8/1/1974.
2. Copy of original from Liam Deasy personal documents.
3. First, four prisoners were executed, then following Erskine Childers' arrest, 10 November and found in possession of a small revolver given to him as a gesture of friendship by Michael Collins; he was tried by court-martial (emergency powers) and executed by firing squad 16 November 1922.
4. Liam Deasy private papers.
5. Ernie O'Malley, *On Another Man's Wound*, p. 299.
6. *Ibid.*
7. Seán Cronin, *The McGarrity Papers*, p. 133.
8. Lynch to McGarrity – Seán Cronin, *The McGarrity Papers*, p. 134.
9. Letter to Con Moloney, 26 January 1922.
10. General Order No. 9, 27 September 1922.
11. Captured documents, File P7/A/82. Mulcahy papers, University College, Dublin, Archives.
12. Captured documents, File P7/A/83. *Ibid.*
13. *Ibid.*
14. Memo, No. 7, dated 4 December, 1922, P7/A/85, Mulcahy papers, University College, Dublin, Archives.
15. *Freeman's Journal*, 16 March 1923; also quoted P. S. O'Hegarty, *The Victory of Sinn Féin*, pp. 205–9.
16. Letter to 'Comrade' 9 February 1923. Mulcahy papers, University College, Dublin, Archives, P7/A/84 also P7/A/85.
17. Florence O'Donoghue, *No Other Law*, p. 291.
18. See Appendix III.
19. See also letter, 9 February 1923, Florence O'Donoghue, *No Other Law*, p. 293.
20. Lynch private family papers.
21. Liam Deasy, author interview, 5/12/1972.
22. P. J. Ruttledge to De Valera, 7 February 1923.
23. Todd Andrews. author interview, 4/11/1983; Liam Lynch to De Valera, Longford and O'Neill, *Éamon de Valera*, p. 215.
24. Longford and O'Neill, *Éamon de Valera*, p. 216.
25. Todd Andrews, author interview, 4/11/1983.

With Executive members

1. Captured documents, P7a/199, Mulcahy papers, University College Dublin, Archives; see also *Irish Independent*, 9 April 1923.
2. Mulcahy papers, University College, Dublin, Archives, P7a/199.
3. In First Southern Division relative strength: Republicans 1,270; Free State, 9,000; Southern Command – Counties: Cork, Kerry, Limerick, Clare, Tipperary, Kilkenny, Carlow, Wexford, and approximately half Galway, 6,800 Republicans; Free State 15,000. Total Free State combat troops 38,000 approximately.
4. Lynch to Con Moloney, 29 March 1923.

5. Todd Andrews, *Dublin Made Me*, p. 280.
6. Captured documents, P7a/199, Mulcahy papers, University College Dublin, Archives.
7. Signatures of Canon Ryan, adm. Thurles; Rev. P. O'Leary, CC, Cork. Rev. Tom Duggan; Frank Daly, chairman Cork Harbour Board; G. P. Dowdall and Dr Tadgh O'Donovan, Cork; Most Rev. D. Harty, Cashel.
8. *Irish Independent*, 8 March 1923.
9. Todd Andrews, author interview, 4/11/1983.
10. *Ibid.*
11. Seán McSwiney; Michael Crowley, Liam Riordan, Peter Donovan, Ned Fitzgibbon, Seán Cotter and Denis Galvin. A lorry driven by Michael Lucy took them to Bweening; Batt Walshe, Tadgh Mullane and Jim McCarthy took them to Jack O'Sullivan's.
12. Todd Andrews, *Dublin Made Me*, p. 212.
13. Lynch was feeling sick, so he gave £5 to Todd Andrews and asked him to remain in Araglin until the return of the members.

Death on the Knockmealdowns
1. 'De Valera was not however at first admitted to the meeting. He waited impatiently in another room while the members of the Executive decided whether or not they would allow him to attend', Longford and O'Neill, p. 217.
2. Meeting held – 24, 25, 26 March 1922.
3. Seán Cronin, *The McGarrity Papers*, 21 December 1922, p. 133.
4. *Ibid.* p. 135.
5. T. Ryle Dwyer, *De Valera's Darkest Hour*, p. 139.
6. *For*: Tom Barry, Tom Crofts, Seán Dowling, Humphrey Murphy, Seán McSwiney; *Against*: Liam Lynch, Frank Aiken, Tom Derrig, Seán Hyde, Austin Stack, Bill Quirke.
7. One of the signatories of the 1916 Proclamation – had been jailed previously in England – solitary confinement with hands tied behind his back so that he had to eat his food like an animal.
8. Gallagher papers, MS 18,375(6), National Library of Ireland, Archives.
9. Those who used this hiding place were often given meals in O'Brien's, Treacy's and O'Gorman's and other houses in the locality.
10. Michael Condon and Bill Houlihan were on duty at Goatenbridge; Ned Looney and Jim Burke on the Clogheen road; Tom McGrath and Michael Donnell at approach from Newcastle.
11. Maurice Twomey in an interview for *Evening Herald*, 2 February 1972 – Interview taken from a series of articles compiled by P. J. Donaghy, Ned Murphy and Joe Kennedy.
12. Florence O'Donoghue, *No Other Law*, p. 305.
13. *Ibid.* See also *Evening Herald*, 2 February 1972.
14. Ned Murphy recalls interview with Frank Aiken. See also *Evening Herald*, 31 January, 1 and 2 February 1972.
15. Statement written by Lieut Clancy – copy Lynch private family papers.

16. *Ibid.*
17. *Ibid.* Details of a document which was prepared by Lieut Clancy and came into the possession of the *Evening Herald* – Article-series compiled by Ned Murphy, Joe Kennedy and P. J. Donaghy, 31 January, I February, 2 February 1972. Copy of the Clancy document in the Lynch family papers.

Inquest and final resting

1. *An Phoblacht*, Saturday 10 April, 1922.
2. Florence O'Donoghue, *No Other Law*, p. 305.
3. Seán Hyde, author interview, 13/7/1974.
4. *The Clonmel Nationalist*, 14 April 1923.
5. *The Clonmel Chronicle*, 14 April 1923; *Sunday Telegraph* 12 April, 1923.
6. *Irish Independent*, 14 April 1923.
7. De Valera to P. J. Ruttledge, 11 April, 1923, quoted by Longford and O'Neill, p. 219. See also T. Ryle Dwyer, *De Valera's Darkest Hour*, p. 139.
8. De Valera to Austin Stack, 10 April 1923, as quoted by Longford and O'Neill, p. 219; see also T. Ryle Dwyer, *De Valera's Darkest Hour*, p. 139.
9. Inquest – Clonmel Coroners' District, 11/4/1923, Public Records Office, Dublin.
10. Inquest – Clonmel Coroners' District, 11/4/1923, Public Records Office, Dublin. See also the *Irish Independent*, 14 April 1923.
11. *Ibid.*
12. *Irish Independent*, 15 April 1923.
13. *The Cork Examiner*, 13 April, 1923; *Irish Independent*, 13 April 1923.
14. *Irish Independent*, 13 April 1923.
15. *Ibid.*, 13 April 1923.
16. *The Clonmel Chronicle*, 14 April 1923.
17. *The Weekly Examiner*, 21 April 1923.
18. *The Weekly Examiner*, 21 April 1923.
19. *Irish Independent*, 14 April 1923.
20. 'Let no man write my epitaph ... When my country takes her place among the nations of the earth, then and not till then, let my epitaph be written. I have done' – Robert Emmet before he was executed on 20 September, 1803.

Bibliography

Primary Sources

University College, Dublin, Archives
Richard Mulcahy Papers
Ernie O'Malley Papers and Notebooks

National Library of Ireland
J. J. O'Connell Papers
Frank Gallagher Papers
Luby Papers
Joseph McGarrity Papers

Public Records Office, Dublin
Clonmel Coroners' Report

Private Papers
The Liam Lynch Family Papers and letters, held by Biddy O'Callaghan
Ned Murphy Private Papers
Paddy O'Brien collection
Bill McKenna correspondence.
Liam Deasy Private Papers
Dan (Sando) O'Donovan documents

Oral Testimony
Interviews with a number of people as listed in the acknowledgments and notes.
Many of these people were directly involved in the Movement and events of the
time.

Newspapers, Periodicals & Journals.
Irish Times; Irish Independent; Irish Press; Freeman's Journal; Cork Examiner;
Cork Co. Eagle; Cork Weekly Examiner; Evening Echo; Cork Constitution;
Evening Herald; The Times; Sunday Independent; Sunday Press; The Evening
Press; Melbourne Irish News; Clare Champion; Limerick Leader; Southern Star;
The Kerryman; The Clonmel Nationalist; The Clonmel Chronicle; An tÓglach;
An Phoblacht; Capuchin Annual; Clare Champion; Kerryman Supplements;
Southern Star Supplements; Irish News; Catholic Bulletin.

Secondary Sources
Andrews, C. S. *Dublin Made Me*, The Mercier Press, Dublin & Cork, 1979.
Barry, Tom, *Guerilla Days in Ireland*: Dublin 1949.
— *The Reality of the Anglo-Irish War 1920–21 in West Cork: Refutations,*
    Corrections and Comments on Liam Deasy's Towards Irish Free, Tralee
    1974.
Beaslaí, Piaras, *Michael Collins and the Making of a New Ireland*, Vols 1 & 2,
    Dublin 1926.

Bell, J. Bowyer, *The Secret Army*, London 1970.
Bennett, George, *The History of Bandon*, Cork 1869.
Bowman, John, *De Valera and the Ulster Question 1917–73*, Oxford 1982.
Bennett, Richard, *The Black and Tans*, London 1970.
Breen, Dan, *My Fight for Irish Freedom*, Tralee 1964.
Brennan, Robert, *Allegiance*, London 1950.
Butler, Ewan, *Barry's Flying Column*, London 1972.
Carroll, Joseph T., *Ireland in the War Years, 1939–1945*, London 1975.
Chavasse, Moirin, *Terence MacSwiney*, London 1961.
Comerford, Máire, *The First Dáil*, Dublin 1969.
Coogan, Tim Pat, *Ireland since the Rising*, London 1966.
— *The I.R.A*, London, 1971.
Cronin, Seán, *The McGarrity Papers*, Tralee, 1972.
Crowley, Flor, *In West Cork Long Ago*, Dublin & Cork, 1979.
Crozier, Brigadier General F.P. , *Ireland Forever*, London 1932.
Dalton, Charles, *With the Dublin Brigade (1917–1921)*, London 1929.
Deasy, Liam, *Towards Ireland Free*, Dublin & Cork 1973.
— *Brother Against Brother*, Dublin & Cork 1982.
Dwyer, T. Ryle, *Éamon de Valera*, Dublin 1980.
— *Michael Collins and The Treaty: His Difference with De Valera*, Cork 1981.
Farrell, Brian, *The Founding of Dáil Eireann: Parliament and Nation-Building*, Dublin 1971.
— *The Creation of the First Dáil*, Dublin 1974.
Figgis, Darrell, *Recollections of the Irish War*, London 1927.
Fitzpatrick, David, *Politics and Irish Life, 1913–21: Provincial Experience of War and Revolution*, Dublin 1977.
Forester, Margery, *Michael Collins: The Lost Leader*, London 1971.
Gaughan, J. A., Austin Stack: *Portrait of a Separatist*, Dublin 1977.
Greaves, C. D., *Liam Mellows and the Irish Revolution*, London 1971.
Hogan, David, *Four Glorious Years*, Dublin 1953.
Kee, Robert, *Ourselves Alone: The Green Flag*, Vol 3. London 1973.
Keyes, Kathleen, *There is a Bridge at Bandon*, Cork & Dublin 1972.
Langford, Siobhán, *The Hope and the Sadness*, Cork 1980.
Lee, Joseph & Ó Tuathaigh, Gearóid, *The Age of de Valera*, Dublin 1982.
Limerick's Fighting Story, Tralee 1949.
Longford, Earl of, and O'Neill, Thomas P., *Éamon De Valera*, Dublin 1970.
Lyons, F. S., *Ireland Since the Famine*, London 1973.
Macardle, Dorothy, *The Irish Republic*, London 1968.
— *Tragedies of Kerry*, Dublin 1924.
Mac Eoin, Uinseann, *Survivors*, Dublin 1980.
Macready, General Sir Nevil, *Annals of an Active Life*, 2 vols. London 1924.
Manning, Maurice, *The Blueshirts*, Dublin 1970.
McCann, John, *War by the Irish*, Tralee, 1946.
Murphy, John A., *Ireland in the Twentieth Century*, Dublin 1975.
Neeson, Eoin, *The Civil War in Ireland, 1921–1923*, Cork & Dublin 1966.
Neligan. Dave, *The Spy in the Castle*, London 1968.
Ó Broin, Leon, *Revolutionary Underground: The Story of the Irish Republican Brotherhood, 1858–1924*, Dublin 1976.

O'Callaghan, Seán, *Execution*, London 1974.
O'Connor, Batt, *With Michael Collins in the Fight for Irish Independence*, London 1929.
O'Connor, Ulick, *A Terrible Beauty is Born*, London 1975.
— *Oliver St. John Gogarty*, London 1981.
O'Donoghue, Denis, J., *A History of Bandon*, Cork 1970.
O'Donoghue, Florence, *No Other Law*, Dublin 1956.
— *Thomas MacCurtain*, Tralee, 1971.
O'Donovan Rossa, Diarmuid, *Rossa's Recollections*, Shannon 1972.
Ó Dúlaing, Donncha, *Voices of Ireland*, Dublin 1984.
O'Malley, Ernie, *On Another Man's Wound*, Tralee 1979.
— *The Singing Flame*, Tralee, 1979.
O'Farrell, Patrick, *Ireland's English Question*, London 1971.
O' Hegarty, P. S. *The Victory of Sinn Féin*, Dublin 1924.
Ó Suilleabháin, Micheál, *Where Mountainy Men Have Sown*, Tralee 1965.
Parkenham, Frank, *Peace by Ordeal*, London 1972.
Rebel Cork's Fighting Story, Tralee 1963.
Ryan, Desmond, *Seán Treacy and the Third Tipperary Brigade, IRA*, Tralee 1945.
Ryan, Meda, *The Tom Barry Story*, Dublin & Cork 1982.
Taylor, Rex, *Michael Collins – The Big Fellow*, London 1961.
Townshend, Charles, *The British Campaign in Ireland 1919–1921*, Oxford 1975.
Walsh, Joe, *The Story of Dick Barrett*, Cork 1972.
— *The Story of Liam Lynch*.
Walsh, J. J. *Recollections of a Rebel*, Tralee 1949.
Younger, Calton, *Ireland's Civil War*, London 1972.
Who Was Who, 1961–1970, London 1979.
With the IRA in the Fight for Freedom: 1919 To the Truce, Tralee 1955.

Index

TOM BARRY

IRA FREEDOM FIGHTER

Meda Ryan

They said I was ruthless, daring, savage, bloodthirsty, even heartless ... the clergy called me and my comrades 'murderers'. But the British were met with their own weapons – they had gone down in the mire to destroy us and our nation, and down after them we had to go.

Tom Barry chronicles the action-packed life of the Commander of the Third West Cork Flying Column and one of the great architects of modern guerrilla warfare in Ireland's fight for freedom. 'The false surrender' controversy, during the decisive Kilmichael ambush, is brought into sharp focus, as is the controversy regarding sectarianism during the 1920–1922 period.

The story of Tom Barry's life, peppered by his battles with the State and Church and his constant endeavours to obtain an All-Ireland Republic, makes him a unique and important figure of Irish history.

Tom Barry details his involvement on the fringes of the treaty negotiations; his Republican activities during the Civil War; his engagement in the cease-fire/dump arms deal of 1923; his term as the IRA's chief-of-staff and his participation in IRA conflicts in the 1930s, 1940s and 1950s, right up to his death in 1980.

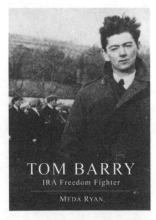

TOM BARRY
IRA Freedom Fighter
MEDA RYAN